W9-DEC-876

You-Can-Do-It

CE National, Inc.
1003 Presidential Dr.
P. O. Box 365
Winona Lake, IN 46590

While CE National is happy to make resources available for believers, CE National does not necessarily endorse the contents or views of the authors of these materials.

FaMiLy MiNiStry EvEntS

Building Faith and Community in the Families of Your Church

by Susan Martins Miller

Standard® PUBLISHING
Bringing The Word to Life

Cincinnati, Ohio

You-Can-Do-It Family Ministry Events

Published by Standard Publishing, Cincinnati, Ohio
www.standardpub.com

Copyright © 2007 by Susan Martins Miller

All rights reserved. No part of this book may be reproduced in any form, except for brief quotations in reviews, without the written permission of the publisher.

Printed in U.S.A.

Credits
Cover design: Grannan Graphic Design
Interior design: Grannan Graphic Design
Editorial team: Dawn Medill, Ruth Frederick, Lu Ann Nickelson

All Scripture quotations, unless otherwise indicated, are taken from the HOLY BIBLE, NEW INTERNATIONAL VERSION®. NIV®. Copyright © 1973, 1978, 1984 by International Bible Society. Used by permission of Zondervan Publishing House. All rights reserved.

13 12 11 10 09 08 07   5 4 3 2 1

0-7847-1976-4

Table of Contents

INTRODUCTION

Dan and Karen moved to a new town and visited several churches. One in particular had a strong ministry to families with younger children. Dan and Karen had younger children but they also had a teenager, and after one visit to the youth group he decided this was not for him. Dan and Karen kept looking.

Diane had seven children. She moved frequently with her common-law husband. Somewhere along the way, she began an exciting journey with Jesus. But her husband didn't. The car didn't always work, and when it did, Raymond needed it. If Diane wanted to go to church, she had to walk with seven children, so her options were limited. Every week she walked to the nearest church.

Derrick was in the military, and his family moved every three years as he was reassigned. They learned to jump in quickly in new places and make friends fast. They didn't have a year to spend looking for a place to belong.

Raynelle had a messy divorce and a demanding work schedule. But she wanted her kids to go to church when she could get them there.

Jeff and Amy were burned out in a church they belonged to for 12 years. Their family life had paid a price for their leadership involvement. Now, in a new church, they wanted to take it slow and easy. The back pew was plenty comfortable for now.

Janet remembered going to church as a child. Everything seemed peaceful; at least that's the way she remembers it. Now she's stressed out with kids of her own, and she wonders if church is still a place of peace.

Every family has its own fingerprint. They don't all look alike. They carry varying amounts of emotional baggage and family secrets. Stress triggers a range of responses, from instant panic to surprising nonchalance. Statistics abound about teenage pregnancy, single parents, cohabiting couples, divorces, and blended families. It's difficult to draw any lines around the shape of today's family.

But families are still made up of individuals, and individuals still have social, emotional, and spiritual needs. Individuals need a safe place to belong, the place they can always go back to no matter how much they mess up, and the place where they are always welcome. People thrive when they know somebody loves them, when they feel less alone.

Family ministry can be the portal into the church for the ready-to-jump-in families as well as the testing-the-waters families. It's more than programs to attend. It's more than making sure there's a class for every age and the nursery is well staffed. Strong family ministry looks at the underlying needs of families—relationship, belonging, acceptance, encouragement, authenticity, partnership—and considers how the church can help meet those needs. Family ministry can't meet every need of every family. But it can help make the church the place where people can bring their needs without fear of judgment or rejection. It can lead the charge for churches to partner with parents in the spiritual formation of their children. It can remind the church of the primacy of family relationships and how essential it is that these relationships be healthy.

But all that can seem overwhelming! What is the children and family ministry director supposed to do?

This book doesn't answer every question we might raise about family ministry. It's not about theory or studies or academic perspectives. All those things have their places. But this book is meant to help you know that you can make a difference. You can facilitate the kind of relationships and environment that give families a healthy context for growing and learning. You can help families build their own spiritual frameworks. You can help them pray together, read the Bible together, listen to each other, think beyond themselves. You can help families connect with other families in genuine ways.

You'll find a brief section that lays a foundation for family ministry. After that, the book is hands-on.

Explore 20 various family ministry events that are easy to carry out. Step-by-step instructions lead you through the process. The not-so-hidden agenda is to help parents discover they really can make spiritual connections with their kids, to help families connect with other families, and to make everyone feel secure in the larger faith family—kids and adults, individuals and all sorts of families. Use the "Take It Home" section to wrap up each gathering with a brief devotional time that all ages can participate in.

Twelve Faith Foundations help parents have brief, successful experiences making spiritual connections with their kids at home. These are reproducible pages that you can use any way that seems to fit your ministry.

Twenty-four brief articles provide a reproducible resource for letting families know you're tuned into their challenges. Put them in bulletins, newsletters, or special mailings—anything that works for you.

I write with the prayer that this book helps put family ministry within reach for you and that it is an encouragement to your vision for touching the lives of families in your congregation and community.

Susan Martins Miller

Why Family Ministry?

What is family? Ask a hundred people, you'll get a hundred answers. Some answers will be full of warm fuzzies, some full of hostile barbs. The traditional family unit of a husband and wife, and children, if God so blesses them, is not nearly as typical as it used to be. Yet studies consistently point to the benefits of children growing up with a mother and father in a family that stays together. Individuals are wounded in their own families—and in their church families—yet they continue to crave a sense of belonging and acceptance.

God created us with that craving. Ultimately He wants us to belong to Him. God created the family, and in the family we have the opportunity to model the kind of belonging and acceptance that God offers us. But the woundedness we all carry gets in the way. That's why we need family ministry. We have great intentions for what we want our families to be like, but we fall short. That's why we need family ministry. The church, the family of faith, is in a position to model the kinds of relationships of grace and encouragement that are healthy for families. The family of faith helps individual families be the best they can be.

James and Mare counted down the days to the birth of their third son. Finally the birth pangs began. But something went wrong during delivery. Little Luke never saw the light of this world. Now James and Mare hardly know how to talk to each other and their little boys don't understand what happened.

Shari landed a great new job at a Christian organization. She worked hard through the first week, trying to get her bearings and come out of the gate running. On Monday of the second week, she did not come in to work. Or Tuesday. Or Wednesday. Or ever. Her husband did not want her to work and had badly beaten her over the weekend.

Sarah was eight-months pregnant with her second child when her husband told her he was homosexual. Getting married had been a mistake, he said, and he needed to leave.

Jack had a high-paying job, and he and Julie lived up to the standard they thought would last forever. But Jack lost his job. He lost his house. He almost lost Julie and the kids.

Laurie's parents divorced when she was a baby. Her mother remarried and divorced twice more. Now Laurie has a husband and daughter of her own. But she is terrified that she won't do any better at providing a stable home.

Jamie, 16, had a new boyfriend. Her parents liked him quite a lot, but they insisted that if Andy wanted to see Jamie, he had to attend church with the family. One day her mother found a prescription for prenatal vitamins in Jamie's jeans.

Jason held his little sister's hand and followed his mother across the parking lot and through the familiar doors. He knew where everything was at the food pantry. They went every month.

The family is in crisis.

More than half of all marriages break up, and statistics are not much different within the church. Kids are not sure where "home" is. Today's married adults juggle a two-income schedule—because of financial need, vocational calling, or personal ambition—with the time and attention it takes to nurture healthy children in a secure home. Blended families, increasing in number every year, don't have a good roadmap. Debt overwhelms families as they chase the American dream—causing more stress and an environment ripe for crisis. Generation X—young adults born between 1965 and 1981—are at a stage of life of building their own families. Some have teenagers, some toddlers. No matter what stage of family they are in, they share a generational experience: the first generation of latch-key kids whose parents often were not around; 50 percent have parents who divorced; a fast-paced childhood; separation from extended family.

Even apart from major stress factors, people and families go through various predictable stages: childhood, adolescence, dating and premarital years, early married years, child-rearing years, empty-nest season, retirement. The needs of the family vary and ministry to the family changes according to the particular stage. These transitions aren't always easy. Toddlers and teenagers alike have a reputation for being difficult. Raising children is consuming and exhausting. Marriage takes work. It's a delicate balance that is easily upset. Prolonged illness, the loss of a child at any age, financial distress, major geographical moves, aging parents, teen sexuality and unplanned pregnancy—any one of these stressors impacts the family significantly, and many families deal with multiple stress factors.

Enter the Church

What can the church do? What *should* the church do?

The church is in the business of helping people become more like Christ. This includes their family relationships at all stages. Churches recognize that they are in a strategic position to minister to families—to help them be whole and healthy before crisis hits, perhaps avoiding it altogether. They are in a strategic position to be the safety net of community and faith encouragement that this generation yearns for.

Most often all the members of a family go to church together. They don't play soccer together, they don't sing in a community choir together, they don't go to night school together, and they don't go to work together. But they do go to church together, which puts the church in a great position to minister to the whole family. The church can influence families during the life transitions they expect and the stress factors they don't expect.

Much of family life is routine, mundane even. You get up in the morning and get the kids to daycare or school, then go to work yourself. In the afternoon you pick everyone up and return home to the task of putting a meal on the table, starting a load of laundry, helping with history homework, and getting to T-ball practice on time. Tomorrow you do it again. Next week you do it again. Even the pressure of maintaining this routine can become a stress factor.

But God uses the routine, the mundane. Think about James and John, or Peter and Andrew. They were fishermen going about their business. Repairing nets certainly doesn't make the list of top ten most exciting things to do. Jesus spoke right into this daily routine and called people to become his closest followers and leaders of the early church.

Mary and Martha weren't doing anything particularly exciting when Jesus decided to visit. In fact, we might say that Martha was much too caught up in the routine. When she complained that Mary wasn't helping her with all the work, Jesus told Martha to take a break! Realize what is important—and it's not the dishes and cooking.

While traveling through Samaria, Jesus stopped at a well at the hottest part of the day. Normally no one would be at the well, coming instead in the morning or evening when the temperature was cooler. But one woman maintained a routine of going to the well at the heat of the day because she was a social outcast and intentionally avoided contact with more respectable women. Jesus met her there with a message that changed her life.

A Roman officer pleaded with Jesus for the life of his daughter, and Jesus brought her back to life. A tax collector climbed a tree, and Jesus paused in the road to look up and talk to him.

In His parables, a primary tool in His teaching, Jesus used ordinary objects and characters—a lost coin, a lost sheep, seeds in a field, a wedding feast, travelers, servants and masters, fathers and sons, tenants and owners.

Jesus used the most ordinary parts of life to transform the lives of the people who listened to Him. Why should things be different now? Jesus still uses the most ordinary parts of our lives to transform us. The church tells this good news! The church tells families that Jesus is with them, that Jesus cares. The church tells families that Jesus can make them strong, no matter what.

In Christ's Light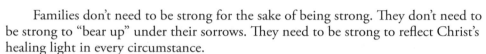

Families don't need to be strong for the sake of being strong. They don't need to be strong to "bear up" under their sorrows. They need to be strong to reflect Christ's healing light in every circumstance.

The number of U.S. families that fit the traditional two-parent-and-children mold is shrinking. That's not news. This kind of family will likely be in the minority in the twenty-first century. Families tend to be smaller. Marriage and family roles look different than they used to. The sad truth is that Christian families are not any less likely to crumble than any other family. Some parents are on their own with the kids. Grandparents are raising their children's kids. Second marriages often bring blended families. The family just doesn't look like it used to—or what we think we want it to look like. But these are real families, and they need to be strong. Family relationships go with us through our whole lives, despite separations and other obstacles. Family is where we belong, where we are known, and look out for each other.

A strong family is not one that doesn't have problems or never faces a crisis. Stressors affect all families in some form or another. Family strength, instead, is how the family meets those challenges and finds their way through a crisis. Life on the other side of the crisis tunnel will not look like it did before. The family must adapt, rebound, and get back on its feet.

Here the church can help. Churches are a prime setting for genuine relationships and authentic community. A church like this becomes a safe place for the family to be, whether in crisis, recovering from crisis, or enjoying a relatively stable season. In the church, people help people they love.

Even more, the church can be a place of prevention. In times of crisis, we offer each other high levels of care and support. If we offer these same high levels *before* the crisis strikes, we make the family strong.

Family ministry is not about information. Certainly information helps; it's one way for people to understand what's happening to them and around them. But on a much larger level, family ministry is about transformation. When someone is in a crisis and emotions are running strong and high, information is not likely to sink in. But relationships will. Relationships bridge the gap between alienated lostness and embracing support structure.

Illness may strike suddenly, or an accident may change the future in a split second. But relational crisis usually begins with little things and sends up warning flares. The unforgiven slight. The offense of criticism. The ears closed to pleas for acknowledgement. Emotions stuffed and compacted for years. What happens to the fundamental relationships within the family during crisis? Family members can either turn to each other for loving support or unleash a host of unrelated anger into an already stressful situation. If family relationships are not intact, any loss or transition has the power to destroy the family.

More Than an Ounce of Prevention

Let's face it; many families are accidents waiting to happen. The balance of things is so fragile that the slightest touch will send everything tumbling. Finances are on edge, relationships are strained, and illness is just around the corner—collisions change lives in a matter of seconds. The government has some programs that help; communities offer the best support they can with limited resources. Families find help for food or childcare or financial counseling or state aid for massive medical bills. But these efforts come into play after the damage is done. The church is in a position to support and strengthen families preventively. It doesn't take a lot of imagination to speculate what might happen to families in your church or community. Divorce happens. Injury happens. Illness happens. Unemployment happens. Death happens. Why should we wait until these travesties strike before stepping in? Why should we act surprised when they do? Rather, the church should expect these things to happen and prepare families to weather them.

Family ministry anticipates. Family ministry looks ahead. Family ministry prepares individuals and families to respond in positive, healthy ways to the inevitable stress factors that every family faces. Family ministry helps families be at their best so they can call on God's strength with faith when those times hit.

Families at their best embrace and live out a growing relationship with Jesus. Parents model what it means to belong to Christ and to live in Christlike ways. Children see this and feel secure. This foundation is essential when crisis hits, and the church can help build this foundation.

Families at their best know how to form and sustain lasting, healthy relationships. They understand forgiveness, encouragement, sacrificial love, humility, and patient prayer at work in relationships within the household. The church—the body of Christ—can be a picture of all these things as members relate to each other in healthy ways as a family of faith.

Families at their best communicate effectively. It's safe to say how you feel, to make your needs known. Families at their best foster an atmosphere of support, not criticism, of self-discipline, not self-indulgence. The church addresses these needs with both overt instruction and model relationships.

Families at their best recognize when they're in trouble. They know when they're sliding off the mark and willingly ask for help. The church must be a safe place to go for help without fear of judgment. God is a refuge; how can His people be anything less?

Families at their best know they are not alone. People at church can be ready to listen, to make sure families know who to call, to connect families with others who have faced a similar stressful season.

Family ministry that anticipates and prepares increases the likelihood that individuals and families will respond in healthy, faith-filled ways when they face transition or loss or discouragement. The goal of family ministry is to create deep connections to God that will pull people into God's care when they need it most. God's grace applies to every situation. Finding it should be no mystery, no theological conundrum. Effective family ministry is the gateway.

What Does God Think About the Family?

God is our Father.
Jesus is our brother.
We are children of God.
The church is the bride of Christ.
The psalmist likens a soul quieted before God
    to a child safe with its mother.
Sounds like a family!
Marriage and family were God's ideas.
After creating Adam, God said,

> "It is not good for the man to be alone.
> I will make a helper suitable for him" (Genesis 2:18).

God created a spectacular world with abundant wildlife and beauty. Adam named every kind of flora and fauna, bird and beast. "But for Adam no suitable helper was found" (Genesis 2:20). So God created Eve, bone from Adam's bones, flesh from Adam's flesh. The connection doesn't get any closer than that. The writer of Genesis recognized the centrality of marriage.

> "For this reason a man will leave his father and mother and be united to his wife, and they will become one flesh" (Genesis 2:24).

Jesus later honored marriage by attending a wedding in Cana (John 2:12), and in fact the occasion of this marriage became the occasion of His first miracle, turning water into wine for the celebration.

A new family unit begins with each marriage. God created Adam and Eve in His own image and told them to be fruitful and multiply—to increase in number (Genesis 1:28). Throughout the Old Testament, Scripture portrays children as a blessing from God—and more is better.

> "Like arrows in the hands of a warrior are sons born in one's youth
> Blessed is the man whose quiver is full of them" (Psalm 127:4, 5).

Relationships are primary to God. Humans were the crowning work of God's creation. These creatures bore God's own image, and He could have a relationship with them that He did not have with the butterflies and daffodils. God gave Adam and Eve a lush, bountiful garden to live in and walked in the garden himself in the "cool of the day" (Genesis 3:8). When He spoke to them, they were not the least bit surprised (Genesis 3:9, 10). God created us to be social and provided immediate relationships with himself and within the family.

God's picture of the family goes even further. He welcomes us into a family of faith, to be children of God himself. We're not servants but sons and daughters.

> **"Yet to all who received him, to those who believed in his name, he gave the right to become children of God"** (John 1:12).

> **"How great is the love the Father has lavished on us, that we should be called children of God! And that is what we are!"** (1 John 3:1).

By His creation of the family unit and by welcoming us into the family of faith, God says that family is important. It's not just something that happened because cave people wanted to keep warm. It didn't evolve as a social convenience. God meant for family to happen—and He made sure it did.

The Family God Had in Mind

Because the family was no accident or coincidence, God makes no secret of what He intends for the family to be. In the Old Testament, God gave parents clear instructions about an important role.

> **"These commandments that I give you today are to be upon your hearts. Impress them on your children. Talk about them when you sit at home and when you walk along the road, when you lie down and when you get up. Tie them as symbols on your hands and bind them on your foreheads. Write them on the doorframes of your houses and on your gates"** (Deuteronomy 6:6-9).

Teaching children to love the Lord is a consuming job. We can't put it in a box to do on Sunday mornings. God wants to see it woven into the fabric of everyday life. Parents, not pastors or Sunday school teachers, are the ones who do this job, knowingly or unknowingly. Family relationships are the context for faith formation.

Honoring parents makes God's "top ten." If any of us tried to distill our value system to ten key points, we'd be fastidiously careful to include the most important and most comprehensive points. The Ten Commandments include the command for children of any age to honor their parents.

> **"Honor your father and your mother, as the Lord your God has commanded you, so that you may live long and that it may go well with you in the land the Lord your God is giving you"** (Deuteronomy 5:16).

God blesses family relationships when we honor one another, especially children honoring parents. He wants parents and children to have a rich, long life together.

In the New Testament, Paul moved beyond theology to practical living and got down to the nitty-gritty—what happens in kitchens and living rooms when families aren't worried that someone is watching.

> "Submit to one another out of reference for Christ. Wives, submit to your husbands as to the Lord. . . . Now as the church submits to Christ, so also wives should submit to their husbands in everything.

> "Husbands, love your wives, just as Christ loved the church and gave himself up for her. . . . In the same way, husbands ought to love their wives as their own bodies. He who loves his wife loves himself.

> "Children, obey your parents in the Lord, for this is right. 'Honor your father and mother'—which is the first commandment with a promise—'that it may go well with you and that you may enjoy long life on the earth.'

> "Fathers, do not exasperate your children; instead, bring them up in the training and instruction of the Lord" (Ephesians 5:21–6:4).

Most of us don't have to think too hard to remember a time our fathers exasperated us! And husbands and wives exasperate each other on a daily basis—sometimes hourly! It's no secret that married couples don't always see eye-to-eye. Once you open the lid on the child-rearing can, you'll never get it back on. Family life is as challenging today as it was in the first century. And Paul's words are just as relevant. Paul clearly lifted family relationships out of the realm of power and authority and dropped them securely in the realm of submission to Christ. What happens in the kitchen or living room when no one is watching is not about who's in charge, but the mutual goal of Christlikeness.

God's idea is that families live together in harmony and love—thinking of others first, honoring each other, sacrificing for each other, building one another other up, worshiping together, sharing in the life of the Spirit. This is the point of Paul's teaching in Ephesians 5. He acknowledged that it could be hard; the fact that he chose to speak to this issue tells us he knew the challenge. As an educated Jew, Paul surely knew the other end of the spectrum:

> "Better to live on a corner of the roof than share a house with a quarrelsome wife" (Proverbs 21:9).

Ephesians 5 and 6 and similar passages make it clear that family living is not always a piece of cake. But we aspire to the love and unity we see in the family portrait that Paul gave us. That's certainly preferable to living with a quarrelsome spouse—or being the quarrelsome spouse!

Acts 16 tells us the brief story of Lydia, a dealer in purple cloth from the city of Thyatira, who worshiped God in Philippi. When Paul arrived in Philippi, Lydia was at the river with other God-fearing women. The Lord opened her heart to respond to the message Paul preached, and Lydia and her entire household were baptized into the faith (Acts 16:13-15). This is a picture of unity in the family. Individual members didn't pick and choose; they converted as a family and embraced the new faith.

Later in the same chapter we read the story of the Philippian jailer. When an earthquake loosened the chains of all the prisoners, the jailer was ready to fall on his own sword. If the prisoners escaped, he would be put to death soon enough anyway. But Paul stopped him. The prisoners were still there. This opened the door for Paul to preach the gospel again, and the jailer believed. Immediately he and all his family were baptized (Acts 16:25-33).

Today we may think the family is going in too many different directions. God points the family in only one direction—toward Him.

When Things Go Wrong and They Will

Submission and love are not always perfect. Family relationships get rocky.

In the very first family, Cain murdered his brother Abel because God found Abel's sacrifice more acceptable than Cain's.

Jacob knowingly and willingly stole his brother's birthright and caused the family feud of all feuds.

Joseph's brothers had their fill of their father's favoritism and took matters into their own hands. They did their best to get Joseph out of the picture permanently.

Hannah was jealous of her husband's other wife, who gave him children while Hannah was barren.

David's sin with Bathsheba brought the death of their child.

David's grown sons jockeyed for the power of the throne even at the price of each other's lives.

The prophet Hosea married an adulterous wife and she did not reform.

Although Ahab was king, he was a whiny wimp. His wife, Jezebel, ran the country not with submission and love, but one calculating play for power.

Herod ruled over Galilee and Perea. John the Baptist denounced Herod's immoral marriage. When Herod's wife and stepdaughter connived to have John the Baptist beheaded, Herod, though distressed, agreed.

The mother of two of Jesus' disciples, James and John, pridefully asked Jesus to give her sons special treatment in the kingdom.

Yes, family relationships get rocky. Sin entered the world when Adam and Eve chose to disobey God in the Garden of Eden, and sin brings pain and sorrow and stress and destruction. The family—even the Christian family—is subject to all these and more.

God Works Through All Kinds of Families

Sin pollutes love and submission, making them worthless without the redeeming grace of God. But God gives his redeeming grace generously. He hasn't given up on the family, and He works through all kinds of families.

Abram and Sarai didn't have children. But Abram needed an heir, a male heir. Sarai says to Abram, "Sleep with my servant. We can have a family through her." In the culture of the day, this was not an unusual suggestion. Abram slept with Hagar and she became pregnant. Unfortunately she lorded it over Sarai and the two of them were soon unable to get along. Hagar decided to run away, but an angel of the Lord told her to go home. God would give her more descendents than anyone could count. Hagar went home, and we read of this adoptive family in Genesis 16. And even though Abram and Sarai, who became Abraham and Sarah, got a little too anxious and took things into their own hands, God miraculously gave them a son of their own and built His people of faith from their descendents.

The prophet Elisha met a widow who was at the end of her rope. She was a single mother with two children to care for with few resources. Her dead husband's creditors were coming to take her sons as slaves because she was unable to pay his debts. Her cupboards were bare except for a little oil. Elisha told her to collect all the empty jars she could find. Then the oil started to flow. She filled jar after jar after jar, then sold the oil to pay the debts and support her children (2 Kings 4:1-7).

Ruth was a widow and a foreigner. But she was devoted to her mother-in-law and traveled with her to Bethlehem. There she met Boaz, who became her second husband. Their son was Obed, and it was through the family line of a second marriage that Jesus was born into the world.

Esther married a Persian king, someone far outside her culture. But this marriage did not give her any official rights or power. She was as subject to the king's whims as anyone else. When the Jewish people living in Persia were threatened with slaughter, Esther mustered the courage to approach the king, unsummoned, and plead for her people. Because of this, God's people were spared.

Timothy's father was an unbelieving Greek, but his mother was a Jewish Christian. Even when he was a small child, his mother and grandmother instructed him in the faith. The child of a religiously mixed marriage grew up to be a strong leader in the first century church. Paul called him "my true son in the faith" (1 Timothy 1:2).

The Bride of Christ

It is clear what God wants families to be. What families deteriorate into is also clear. Some of the greatest figures of faith in the Bible are also the people who made the biggest messes of their lives. And earnest believers continue to make mistakes. But God is persistent and continues to work in and through His people.

Family ministry aims to help families be everything God wants them to be— through instruction, through mentoring, through modeling, through time together, through presence in times of sorrow and transition. We are the body of Christ, each with gifts that build up the body and minister to its members.

We are also the bride of Christ, pictured beautifully in the closing chapters of Revelation when the kingdom of God comes in its fulfillment.

> "Let us rejoice and be glad and give him glory!
> For the wedding of the Lamb has come and his bride has
> made herself ready" (Revelation 19:7).

The imagery of a wedding expresses the loving, joyful, eternal relationship between God and his people and reminds us again that God created the family unit and welcomes us into His family of faith, and He will never leave or forsake us. This family is forever!

Church and Home, Hand in Hand

Nate and Shari rose from the pew and walked to the front of the church. In Shari's arms, little Abigail squirmed. Nate touched his daughter's head, hoping to soothe her into quietness for the brief ceremony soon to begin. The pastor said, "Let us hear the Gospel concerning Jesus and children" and read from Mark 10 the story of Jesus welcoming children.

Then it was time for the promises of the parents and congregation. "Will you as parents, by God's help, dedicate yourselves to the Christian nurture of your child and bring her up in the worship and teaching of the church, that she may come to know Christ as Savior and follow Him as Lord?"

Nate and Shari answered, "We will." The pastor turned to the congregation.

"Will you as members of this congregation dedicate yourselves to be faithful in your calling as members of the body of Christ, so that this child and all other children among you may grow up in the knowledge and love of Christ our Savior?"

"We will."

Often, after a prayer, the pastor holds the baby up for everyone to see.

In the presentation of a child, parents are asking for the blessing of God on their child. In this act, they accept their responsibility for nurturing the child in Christ's love. For the congregation, this is an opportunity to formally welcome the child to their midst, sharing the parents' joy and looking forward to the day the child chooses to express personal faith. But in the words they speak, the congregation also shares in the spiritual nurture of the child.

Are these just words we say in church, or do we mean them? Are Nate and Shari thinking about what they're saying, or are they hoping that Abigail is not going to cry? Does the congregation consider what they say, or are they thinking that this ritual is going to make the service run long?

Family Living, Faith Lessons

The Bible is full of pictures of family—relationships between husbands and wives, parents and children, brothers and sisters. Not every family in the Bible is perfect, but God's grace is not limited to perfect families. Husbands and wives, parents and children, brothers and sisters—we can read the stories in the Bible and see ourselves in the characters, flaws and all. But we also see the grace of God at work in homes and relationships, and we remember that we can experience the same grace.

Family relationships are the setting for so many lessons in Christian living. Within the family we learn what it means to love, what it means to forgive, to sacrifice, to give, to control our tongues, to speak gently, to celebrate. We experience reconciliation and loyalty and the security of mutual submission. Within the family we learn what it is to share good times and bad, to ache and pray for each other, to see God transforming our relationships. The family is a powerful setting for discipleship.

Paul filled his letters with instructions for how family members should relate to each other.

> "Let the peace of Christ rule in your hearts, since as members of one body you were called to peace. And be thankful. Let the word of Christ dwell in you richly as you teach and admonish one another with all wisdom, and as you sing psalms, hymns and spiritual songs with gratitude in your hearts to God. And whatever you do, whether in word or deed, do it all in the name of the Lord Jesus, giving thanks to God the Father through him.
>
> "Wives, submit to your husbands, as is fitting in the Lord.
> Husbands, love your wives and do not be harsh with them.
> Children, obey your parents in everything, for this pleases the Lord.
> Fathers, do not embitter your children, or they will be discouraged"
> (Colossians 3:15-21).

A similar passage appears in Ephesians, a letter Paul wrote for general circulation. Throughout his letters, Paul offered relational wisdom. He knew that families make the spiritual pilgrimage together. They learn from each other and disciple each other. At home, in the family, is where discipleship happens at the most fundamental level.

A Daunting Task

But parents don't always feel up to the job. Believing parents want their children to come to faith and to live in the Spirit. But how do you make sure that happens? Add in the weary factor of parents who come home dragging at the end of the day, only to face making dinner, cleaning up after dinner, helping with homework and doing three loads of laundry. They use a 24-hour pharmacy because they probably won't have a chance to pick up that prescription until 10 o'clock at night.

By the time parents have a moment to focus on the spiritual well-being of their children, they're too tired. And they don't know what to say. They might feel like they don't know the Bible well enough to talk about with it their kids. Or how do you bring up the subject of putting your trust in Jesus? Family devotions just never seem to work. Parents are unprepared, kids are squirrelly, and everyone just wants it over with. Guilt sets in.

So the parents resolve to make sure their kids get to Sunday school more. The teacher will know what to say, won't she?

Parents don't need a list of "You should have . . ." statements. They know they should have. But they didn't, they couldn't.

Parents don't need a list of "This is what you have to do."

Parents don't need more guilt about not spending enough time with their kids, much less not talking about Jesus enough. Two-income families and single-parent families are here. They are not an aberration in our twenty-first century culture. It's a way of life. It's reality that parents work long hours and come home tired. Even stay-at-home parents work long hours and get tired.

What parents need is partnership. They want the church to come alongside them and help them connect with their kids. They want help to succeed in the things they want to do and know they should do. Imagine what could happen if churches did less educating about parental "should haves" and more empowering about parental "can dos." Together, parents and churches can surround kids with God's love.

Traditionally the role of the church in spiritual formation of children has primarily been instruction based in information. This is what the Bible says. Memorize this verse by next Sunday. Kids soon catch on that the answer to every question is "Jesus" or "pray." Churches offered Sunday school, a midweek club, and perhaps a Bible memorization challenge or a reading contest. Today many churches are turning the boat. Information is not everything. If kids learn every story in the Bible but don't have a relationship with Jesus, the job is not done. If kids believe in Jesus as their Savior so they can go to Heaven but don't understand what that means for living in the here and now, the job is not done.

Churches are moving away from classes for children and toward ministering to the whole family as a family. But it's a big boat, and it takes time to turn it. Going from "classes for all ages" to ministry that helps the family be at its best relationally and spiritually is a wide, sweeping turn that causes waves.

Strengthening family ministry does not necessarily mean adding new programs. It's not so much a list of activities as it is a point of view. Being committed to family ministry means looking at everything the church does from the point of view of the impact it has on families, positively and negatively. A congregation that wants to support families will constantly examine all of its activities for how they touch families, whether negatively or positively.

Do families feel welcome? Ray and Lynne visited a large church with their two daughters, 6-year-old Jenna and 3-month-old Emily. They were members of a small church that had seen an exodus of several key families, and now they were concerned that Jenna didn't have much of a peer group at church. One of the attractions of the large church was the reputation of its children's program on Sunday mornings. So Jenna went to the children's ministry and the rest of the family went to worship. Ray and Lynne had barely found seats before they were asked to leave—because they had taken Emily into the service. Children of any age were not allowed in the worship service. They left in tears. They returned to the small church where women would stand in line to hold Emily during the worship service or pace in the back if needed.

Does the church accommodate family needs? One church had committed to have the whole congregation listen to the entire New Testament in three months time. In a board meeting, the pastor proposed a mid-week Bible study and prayer meeting that would focus on the listening segments for each week. He suggested starting at 7:00 p.m. and going for 60 to 90 minutes. A board member asked whether there would be childcare. The pastor hadn't thought that far ahead. Then someone observed that 7:00 was late for families with small children anyway. If they didn't get home until 8:30 or later, young children would be up past their bedtimes. Parents who know what happens to sleep-deprived kids would almost certainly opt to stay home. The start time was changed to 6:00 and leaders made a commitment to keep the meeting to an hour and provide childcare.

Does the ministry bring families together to spread them out throughout the building? Certainly age-appropriate groupings have their place. Offering a class for parents while kids are in a mid-week club or youth meeting is a wonderful enrichment. But it is possible for programs with the best of intentions to keep family members apart rather than help bring them together. Churches that run children's programming concurrent to adult worship, for instance, offer few opportunities for the entire family to worship together. Often the children's ministry team organizes a simple service project for children, while the youth and adults organize more complex projects. Families don't serve together. Children don't see their parents in a service role and learn from that model.

This can be balanced by offering experiences for the whole family together— seasonal events, quarterly family worship services, regular times that offer meaningful activities in which the entire family can participate.

Does the church create ways for families to know each other well? The family comes to church; the kids go to classes and the parents go to worship. Seventy minutes later they're back in the car. The "one-hour family" is a reality in today's churches. Gone are the days where families stayed at church for three hours in the morning and went back again in the evening. The kinds of relational bonds that used to happen naturally from spending time together take more intentional effort. The bonds are not any less essential than they were a generation ago, but churches must cultivate them in various ways.

Does the church tackle the tough topics? For instance, will the church help parents talk to their kids about sex? Most of the time, no, even though everyone agrees that the issue becomes more prominent in our society every year. Too often all we say is "Don't do it," while every other piece of culture is screaming "Do it!" Will the church help parents navigate the ethical questions that become more complex with widespread technology use by teenagers? Will the church help teens find the balance between being in the culture but not swallowed up by it? The teenage years are a common "dropping out" season. Parents can't make teens come to church the way they could when kids were little. Jobs and sports or simply sleep calls to teens more persuasively than the church does. Church leaders shake their heads and say, "It's hard to keep teens in the church"—and don't try!

Homes That Shape

Home is formative. Whether for good or bad, our homes and families of origin shape us. The church can help parents shape their kids by being a home, a church home. At home, family members care about each other. They squabble, but they figure it out. They disagree, but they learn to understand each other. They learn together. They laugh together. They question together. A healthy home is a safe place to go, to be welcome, to belong.

Families need to belong. The church has a great opportunity to become the place that families want to belong. Everyone in the congregation should belong to a family, either by blood relationship or through adoptions within the church. Faith grandparents. Faith aunts and faith uncles. Church can be a place that models the kinds of relationships we want to see in healthy families.

Caring for families is crucial. The church has a unique opportunity to walk alongside families through every stage and phase of life. The same kinds of skills that healthy families use for living together at home, for creating positive, secure relationships, are the skills the church needs to use to make the congregation a vibrant faith family. A church that is committed to family ministry understands this and looks at its entire ministry through the family lens.

Chelsie called her mother from her friend CJ's house. She wanted to stay at CJ's for dinner—again. On the other end of the phone, Chelsie's mother protested that she was eating at CJ's too often. "That's because they actually have family dinners!" Chelsie told her mother adamantly. "We never do." Chelsie's mother would cook a pot of food every couple of days, and family members were free to eat at their own convenience.

What happens when the family doesn't eat together? Doesn't talk? Doesn't play together? Doesn't pray together? Bonds break down. We persuade ourselves it's all right for each family member to take a plate of food and go into a separate room to watch a separate television. By that time we don't have anything to say to each other anyway.

Leaders must ask, "Is this an experience I would want my own family to have?"

Are we coming alongside families by meeting them where they are rather than going to where we think they should be?

Are we coming alongside families by being a family?

"Will you as members of this congregation dedicate yourselves to be faithful in your calling as members of the body of Christ, so that this child and all other children among you may grow up in the knowledge and love of Christ our Savior?"

"We will."

Family Ministry Reaches Out

T here's family, and then there's family.

There's the family with a mom and a dad and some kids. And there's the family with no dad, or a dad that everyone wishes would go away. Or the mom and the step-mom, the dad and the step-dad, and his, hers, and our kids.

There's the family that cares for each other fiercely. And there's the family who never shows emotion.

There's the family that hikes and plays and laughs together. And there's the family that doesn't speak to each other.

There's the family that goes to church together and then goes home and screams at each other.

We want all the families in our churches to be happy, healthy families. We want them to be the kind of families God wants them to be. We want them to be safe from the traps of a sinful world.

But they aren't. And because they aren't, some of them think they're not good enough for the church and stop coming when times get tough. If they told anyone the truth—well, they just can't. So it's better not to go.

But because families aren't whole and happy and healthy, the church is exactly where they need to be.

Despite how we might idealize family, the truth is some of the deepest hurts we bear come from within our families: physical, sexual, and emotional abuse; lack of forgiveness; unresolved arguments rooted in times of loss; emotional distance and the you-don't-matter message it carries; favoritism and injustice; the stabbing words spoken just to get the upper hand; the silent look of disapproval. Wounds don't have to be visible to the rest of the world to slice deep. We want the family to be everything God intends it to be. In the meantime, it's the most likely place for hurt to happen and gives us the greatest opportunity to minister to hurting people.

Welcome Back

Young and middle adults are at a stage of building their own families. Too often they feel estranged from family and the church—if they were even ever part of the church to begin with. Loneliness, alienation, and broken families have heightened the need of this generation for acceptance and belonging. They long for authentic relationships they can count on, not more organized programs. These adults want a lively experience of the gospel, a spiritual depth they likely did not see around them as they grew up. They're looking for the family they never had. And as they have children of their own, they're looking more to the church to show them how to do this parent and family thing.

Carrie interviewed for a position in a church-run childcare center. The director explained that the center was a ministry of the church and asked about Carrie's own faith and church experience. Carrie had grown up in a church, but as a young married couple, she and her husband had not connected to a church. She did not give a convincing account of her own spiritual journey. "But when I have my own kids," Carrie said, "I definitely want them to grow up in the church. I want them to have that."

Through family ministry, the church has the opportunity to welcome back an alienated generation, to reach out to them with a new picture of what family means. A new picture of family leads to a deeper understanding of being part of the family of God.

Reality Needs

Marriages between Christians are just as likely—or more likely—than the general population to end in divorce. We don't want it to be that way. Hearing this makes us squirm and furrow our brows. We pretend we don't know, that it won't happen to the families in our churches. But it's a statistical fact. These Christians have limited choices: admit failure and drop out of the church rather than go and feel shunned; admit failure and stay in the church—as long as the spouse leaves; find another church for a fresh start.

The percentage of Christian teenagers becoming sexually active during high school also is not statistically different than the general population. Quite logically, some of them have babies. It's not easy to go to church when you're 16 and pregnant. It's not easy to go to church when your daughter is 16 and pregnant.

Why? Why is it so hard? What makes it all right for us to allow it to be so hard? Single parents need the church. Parents separated from their children need the church. Adults who remarry and blend families need the church. Faithful parents whose children wander from the faith need the church.

The father of the prodigal son in Luke 15 watched and waited for the day his son would come home. He wasn't waiting to say, "I told you so," or "You have to face the consequences of your choices" or "I hope you learned something from this experience." He was waiting to say, "Welcome home! I love you!" The son only hoped his father might give him a lowly servant's job, but the father would have none of it. This was his son! "Kill the fatted calf! We're going to have a party in a major way!"

We use this story to teach children the never-ending love of God and the forgiveness that always awaits us when we return to him. How can the church offer anything less to its wounded children who tentatively step through the door again? Family ministry can meet these families at the door—or better yet, go out looking for them—and welcome them home. The church has the opportunity to be a place of restoration and healing, of forgiveness and rebuilding.

Many youth and young adults coming to Christ and entering the church come from dysfunctional families. Helping them grow in the faith inevitably includes helping them with family matters. Sometimes family wounds actually stymie spiritual growth. The church is in the perfect position to reveal a new picture of family—a healthy picture of family—by being family to these people in need.

Dale was a pastor with a charismatic personality. He was leading a church with an unusually high number of young adults and university students. Perhaps his personality attracted them initially, but his ministry went much deeper. This was also a generation of broken people—good people who had fathers who were present but silent, or vocal but absent, or just downright difficult to live with. Dale became a father figure to many of these young adults. He and his wife opened their home to them. Family dinners almost always included an extra plate set for whoever might drop in. Dale spent many Friday evenings hanging out with young adults watching a movie and talking about it. Dale's family was a new picture of family for wounded people.

Sandy's father was a passive personality and her mother a controller. She never felt accepted by either of them for who she was; her mother seemed to want her to be someone else and her father didn't seem to notice her. Sandy left home as soon as she could, despite her mother's protests. As a young adult in a church, she met a senior citizen couple who opened their hearts and home to her, and she found herself seeking their advice and looking for ways she could help them in return. In this couple she had the affirming accepting relationship she had never had with her own parents. Sandy found a new picture of family within the church.

Eighteen-year-old Deb had to leave home. Immediately. Abuse within the household had reached unsafe proportions and she couldn't be there. But where would she go? Although she was a legal adult, she was not ready to stand alone emotionally or financially. Travis and Samantha took her into their home to live with them and their daughter. They gave her shelter, both physically and spiritually. They gave her the experience of a healthy family environment, a new picture, a restored foundation from which to launch her own adult life.

Dotty was a married woman with a believing husband, but she noticed that a number of women in her church came alone. Some of them were divorced with or without children, some widowed, some married to husbands who did not attend church. Dotty started a Sunday school class for "women who come alone." In addition to rich Bible study, for years the group was a tight support group to the women who attended. They'd found their own version of family within the church.

By being family to families in the church and giving people new, restorative models of family relationships, congregations empower people to relate to each other as if they are family—because they are. Restored pictures of the family spill beyond the church walls and into the homes of those who discover them. That doesn't happen because of a class or a program. It happens because of relationships—family relationships.

The Church Can

Being a family is hard work. It probably always has been, but each generation feels the burden in distinct ways. Today's parents feel the load of sustaining two incomes (often a financial necessity) or trying to live on one income (sometimes without choice); the unspoken—and usually unjustified—guilt of working mothers; the anxiety about whether parents are offering their children enough enrichments or the right schooling; the chronic fatigue from keeping up with the family calendar. Technology makes everything faster, but since everything's faster, now we do more, not less. The distance from the "simple life" is too great to think of returning there. Culture has swallowed up the family to the point that some of the most out-of-sorts families don't even realize what they're missing.

The church can reach out to these overscheduled, overburdened, overwhelmed families. The church won't have the solution to every family that is financially overcommitted, but it can offer the gift of contentment. The church won't have the answer to every strained relationship, but it can offer the gift of unconditional love. The church can't magically reshape the household schedule, but it can offer the gift of islands of meaningful time that the family can spend together. The church can't control the TV ads and billboards, but it can stand for purity in an impure world so that families will know it is possible.

Families need to know they don't have to go it alone when they face the challenges of culture, that they don't have to be swallowed up by the environment. They can make choices that reflect their values—God's values. The church can be a steadfast picture of God's culture, not in a judgmental manner but in a demonstrative way. When the church lives the culture of Christ, families will naturally carry it into their homes. They'll know they have something solid and stable in a culture where everything changes by the moment.

We Are the Church

We talk about the church and it's easy to start thinking about buildings and denominations and institutions. The church should be doing this or the church should respond to that.

Paul wrote to the congregation of Christians at Corinth about how the church is to function. His language could not be any less institutional.

> "Now the body is not made up of one part but of many. If the foot should say, 'Because I am not a hand, I do not belong to the body,' it would not for that reason cease to be a part of the body. And if the ear should say, 'Because I am not an eye, I do not belong to the body,' it would not for that reason cease to be part of the body. . . . But in fact God has arranged the parts in the body, every one of them, just as he wanted them to be.

> "The eye cannot say to the hand, 'I don't need you!' And the head cannot say to the feet, 'I don't need you!' . . . If one part suffers, every part suffers with it; if one part is honored, every part rejoices with it.

> "Now you are the body of Christ and each one of you is a part of it" (1 Corinthians 12:14-16, 18, 21, 26, 27).

That's not an institution; that's an organism. The church is a dynamic, caring community that recognizes that every part of the body is valuable. Every part of the body deserves healing and restoration.

As the body of Christ, the people of God, we are a picture of family to the world. The way we relate to each other, respect each other, love each other, honor each other, is the presence of Christ in the world.

Family ministry helps families to be at their best before the crisis hits. Family ministry helps families with healing and restoration. Family ministry helps families in the congregation to be stronger as individual units, and as a result of that, they are better witnesses of the love of Christ and the power of the Spirit in their lives. Family ministry goes beyond the church walls.

Families need other families; they can find them at church, in the caring community that is evidence of the grace of God in broken lives.

FaMily MiNistry EVents

Families need time together to keep relationships healthy and stay attuned to each other's needs. Turn the pages, and you'll find 20 family ministry events that help you help families. Members of the same household can enjoy these times together as well as members of the same household of faith. Use these events to strengthen individual families and cement the bonds between families in the congregation.

You'll find seasonal topics, service projects, craft times, story times, silly times, quiet times, and noisy times. Follow the step-by-step instructions to organize each event, enjoy the time together, and then debrief with a Take It Home time that focuses on a Bible verse. You're building lasting memories!

Please-Join-Us Doorknob Hangers

Most people who come to church for the first time do so because someone invited them. Use these crafty doorknob hangers to invite the neighborhood to a church event or just to remind people that you are there, ready to share God's love.

Set It Up

SUPPLIES:

- colored copier paper
- poster board or craft foam
- scissors
- glue
- glitter glue
- copies of Doorknob Hanger templates on page 31
- pens or markers
- bell or buzzer

Optional:

- foam accent shapes, ribbons, stickers, or other decorative items

Do Ahead ❯ Fill in the information on the card on page 31 to create a master. Make lots of copies of the card on colored paper. Make several copies of the doorknob hanger pattern. You might want to cut out a few shapes ahead of time for participants to use as patterns, or they can cut out the patterns when you meet. Kids will enjoy helping you set out supplies on the tables either ahead of time or at the beginning of your session.

Option! ❯ Ask participating families to bring favorite decorating supplies.

Get It Done ❯ 1. **Cut out the patterns.** Cut out the doorknob hanger patterns. Also cut out the invitation cards.

2. **Cut out the doorknob hanger.** Trace around the pattern on poster board or craft foam and cut out the doorknob hanger. Carefully cut from the top edge in to the circle at the top of the doorknob hanger and cut out the circle.

3. **Glue.** Glue the invitation card to the doorknob hanger.

4. **Sign the invitations.** (Optional) On the back of the doorknob hangers you create, write "your friends at" (fill in the name of your church) and sign the first names of members of your family or small group.

5. **Decorate.** Use the glitter glue, foam accent shapes, markers and any other decorative supplies you have available to make the doorknob hanger fun and colorful. Set the finished project aside to dry.

6. **Deliver.** Plan a time when participating families can go out in the neighborhood around the church and leave invitations on door handles.

7. **Clean up.** There's plenty of work for everyone. Send kids around with trash bags to collect scraps from the tables.

8. **Gather your group together.** Enjoy the Take It Home time together. (See below.)

> ## Family Connections
> - Kids express their natural creativity and parents take time to notice.
> - Parents and kids appreciate together their church family.
> - Kids experience inviting someone to church with the security of parents nearby.

Take It Home

> **Bible Verse:** "Do not forget to entertain strangers, for by so doing some people have entertained angels without knowing it" (Hebrews 13:2).

Bring a bell or buzzer that is loud enough for the group to hear. When the group has gathered, ring the bell or press the buzzer several times. Ask: **How do you respond when you hear a sound like this?** The bell or buzzer will remind people of doorbells or telephones or other sounds that tell us we need to pay attention or respond in some way.

We're going to take doorknob hangers around the neighborhood because we want to get people's attention. We want to let them know we're here to share the love of God with them, even if we don't know them. When people visit our church, we want to make sure they feel welcome.

Have a volunteer read Hebrews 13:2. Ring the bell and ask: **Can you think of any Bible stories where people hosted angels and didn't know it?** These stories may be obscure for kids, but it's a great question for adults! (Abraham, Genesis 18; Gideon, Judges 6; Manoah, Judges 13; Abraham's story is probably most well known.) **When Abraham saw three strangers, he hurried to get them water and a meal. They turned out to be messengers from God who told him that he would have a son the next year.**

Ring the bell and ask: **What do you think *entertain* means in Hebrews 13:2?** We don't have to put on a show; God just wants us to show hospitality and make people feel welcome. It doesn't have to be anything fancy.

Ring the bell and say: **Sometimes we're don't take time to talk to people we don't know at church. This verse reminds us that God even wants us to welcome people we don't know.** Ring the bell. **The next time you hear a doorbell, remember that!**

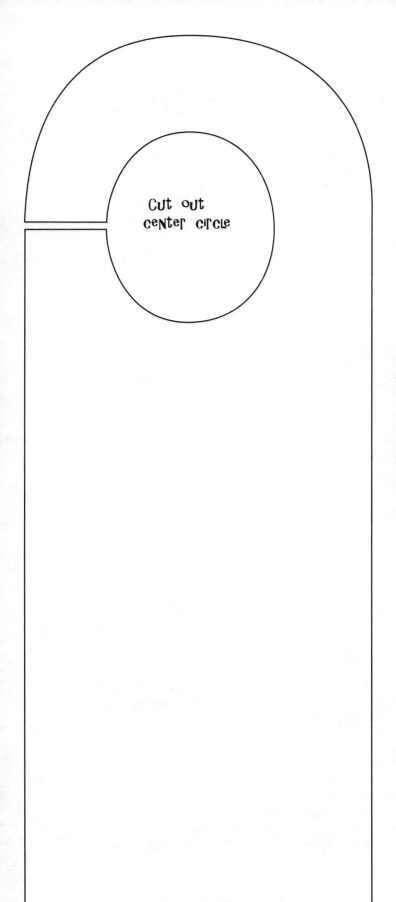

Cut out
center circle

We Want You to Come!

To _____

On _____

At _____

For _____

_____

For more information call:

_____

Copyright © 2007 by Susan Martins Miller. Permission is granted to reproduce this page for ministry purposes only—not for resale.

Cook and Freeze, Ready to Go

A hearty meal hits the spot at times of illness, moving, birth of a baby, or other family transition. Families in your church can enjoy being together as they prepare meals and get them ready to deliver fresh or to freeze for a quick response to future needs in the congregation or community.

Set It Up

Supplies:

- aluminum foil pans and lids
- ingredients for selected recipes
- copies of recipes on pages 34, 35
- mixing bowls and spoons
- measuring cups and spoons
- knives
- stove
- pots
- cleaning supplies
- freezer labels and colorful markers
- water bottle
- plastic container of small treats

Do Ahead ⟫ Photocopy the recipes on pages 34 and 35. Depending on your facilities, you can partially prepare ingredients ahead of time, such as cooking rice or pasta, and assemble dishes as a group. If you have more time and the use of a full kitchen is available, plan to do all the cooking together. Kids will enjoy measuring and pouring. Make sure you have adult supervision for use of the stove and cutting utensils.

Option! ⟫ Ask participating families to contribute ingredients.

Get It Done ⟫ 1. **Set up stations.** For each recipe you plan to prepare, set up a station with all the ingredients and utensils needed. Place a photocopy of the recipe at the station. Plan for groups of four to six people to work at each station. Set up as many stations as needed for the number of people you expect. If your kitchen is small, set up workstations on tables in another area.

2. **Cook and chop.** If you're cooking during your session, have groups begin by measuring water, rice, and pasta. Assign an adult to watch each group's pan on the stove. While the rice or pasta is cooking, the rest of the group can wash and cut vegetables. Lay out everything in the order it's used to assemble the dish.

3. **Assemble.** Follow the recipe to assemble the dish in the casserole or foil pan. Close the lid over the pan or cover securely with aluminum foil. Groups can rotate from one station to another and prepare more than one meal as long as supplies last.

4. **Label.** Use the markers to write on freezer labels the name of the dish, the date it was prepared, and the baking instructions. If you'd like, add another label that says, "Prepared with love for you by . . ." and have group members sign their names.

5. **Get Ready to Deliver.** If you're planning to deliver fresh meals, let groups know where to take their meals. If you're planning to freeze and use the meals later, show groups where to put their meals. Double-check to be sure all meals are properly labeled.

6. **Clean up.** There's plenty of work for everyone!

7. **Gather your group together.** Enjoy the Take It Home time together.

Family Connections

- Kids see parents in a servant's role.
- Parents slow down and realize kids can contribute.
- Families bond during the experience of serving together.
- Families try something they can repeat in their own household to continue serving this way.

Take It Home

Bible Verse: "He satisfies the thirsty and fills the hungry with good things" (Psalm 107:9).

Gather a water bottle and a plastic container of treats. When your group has gathered, hold up the bottle and container. Ask: **How do you feel when you're hungry and thirsty?**

Kids may answer first by describing physical symptoms of discomfort. Adults may realize that physical hunger also affects their mental and emotional state or ability to perform physically. If no one mentions this connection, suggest it yourself.

Pass around the container of treats and let everyone take one. As they munch, ask: **How do you feel after you've had something to eat and drink?** Pause for answers.

Say: **We made some meals to give to people who need them at special times. We all need to eat, and good food helps us to feel better in so many ways. Let's read a Bible verse that talks about being hungry.**

Have a volunteer read aloud Psalm 107:9. Ask: **What does this verse say God does for us?** Listen to answers.

Ask: **What kinds of good things does God fill us with?** Listen to answers.

God knows that we get hungry and thirsty. He knows that we need food for our bodies. But he knows we also need food for our spirits. Only God can give us that. Only God fills us up with good things so we're happy from the inside out.

The next time you're hungry or thirsty, remember to let God fill you up with good things.

Recipe

GROUND BEEF CASSEROLE

1 lb. lean ground beef, browned and drained

1 c. chopped onion

1 can (15 1/2 oz.) diced tomatoes

1 can whole kernel corn, drained

2 c. thinly sliced uncooked potatoes

1/2 c. flour

1 green bell pepper, chopped

1 1/2 c. shredded mild Cheddar or American cheese

Combine beef, onion and tomatoes. In a separate bowl, combine corn, potatoes, flour, and chopped green bell pepper. Layer the beef mixture with the corn and potato mixture. Put the cheese in a resealable bag. Tape the bag securely to the foil lid.

Prepare a baking instruction label and attach it to the foil lid.

Bake uncovered 45 minutes at 375 degrees. Sprinkle with cheese and bake 30 minutes longer.

Recipe

BAKED CHICKEN BREAST

6 portions of boneless, skinless chicken breast

1 can cream of chicken soup

2 c. herb stuffing

1/2 c. water

12 oz. Swiss cheese, grated

1 stick margarine, melted

Place chicken in greased pan. Cover the chicken with Swiss cheese. Mix the water with the soup and pour the mixture over the chicken. Mix the stuffing and margarine. Top the chicken with the stuffing mixture. Prepare a baking instruction label and stick it to the pan lid.

Bake 1 1/2 hours at 325 degrees.

Copyright © 2007 by Susan Martins Miller. Permission is granted to reproduce this page for ministry purposes only—not for resale.

EASY ENCHILADAS

1 lb. ground beef	1 can cream of chicken soup
1/2 c. chopped onion	2 c. grated Cheddar cheese
1/2 c. chopped green pepper	corn tortillas
1 can enchilada sauce	1 can refried beans
8 oz. milk	

Sauté ground beef, onions, and green pepper. Drain fat and set the mixture aside. In a separate mixing bowl, combine enchilada sauce, milk, soup, and 1 cup grated cheese. Soften tortilla shells in microwave for easy rolling. Spread each tortilla with approximately 1 tablespoon of refried beans; then spoon on some of the beef mixture.

Spoon on some of the cheese-soup mixture and roll up the enchilada. Place it in an aluminum foil pan. Repeat until you've used all the tortillas. Pour any extra sauce over the enchiladas. Sprinkle with remaining cheese. Prepare a baking instruction label and stick it to the pan lid.

Bake 30 minutes at 350 degrees.

VEGETARIAN LASAGNA

1 qt. jar spaghetti sauce

2 c. white sauce

2 c. mozzarella cheese

3/4 c. Parmesan cheese

1 pkg. frozen chopped spinach or broccoli

9 uncooked lasagna noodles

To make white sauce: melt 4 Tbsp. margarine and stir in 4 Tbsp. flour, 1/2 tsp. salt and dash of pepper. Cook over medium heat. Gradually stir in 2 cups milk. Heat to boiling, stirring constantly. In a separate pan, cook spinach or broccoli according to directions.

Mix cheeses in a bowl. Spread a little sauce in the bottom of the pan. Layer noodles, spaghetti sauce, spinach or broccoli, white sauce, and cheese mixture. Repeat. Prepare a baking instruction label and stick it on the pan lid.

Bake 45 minutes at 350 degrees.

Copyright © 2007 by Susan Martins Miller. Permission is granted to reproduce this page for ministry purposes only—not for resale.

Waiting for Jesus: Advent

What is Advent about? Advent means "coming." During the Advent season we look forward to celebrating Christ's first coming and look ahead with joy to His second coming. Use this project to give families a practical way to look forward to Christmas while remembering the greatness of God's plan to redeem the world.

Set It Up

Supplies:

- no-bake modeling clay
- raffia or straw
- copies of Advent Readings on pages 38 and 39
- scissors
- thin ribbon or string
- waxed paper
- sturdy paper plates
- resealable sandwich bags

Optional:

- small tent or blanket and chairs

Do Ahead » Photocopy the Advent Readings on tan or pale yellow paper. Purchase no-bake modeling clay or make your own. Adjust this recipe to the number of people you expect: 2 cups salt, 2/3 cup water, 1 cup cornstarch, 1/2 cup cold water. Stir salt and water in saucepan about 5 minutes. Remove from heat and stir in cornstarch and cold water. Allow to cool. Store in resealeable plastic bags until ready to use.

Option! » Add food coloring to the water before adding to the clay mixture.

Get It Done » 1. **Prepare the work surface.** Lay waxed paper over a paper plate for a work surface. This will let you carry the project home before it has dried completely.

2. **Make a clay manger.** Mold clay into a manger shape that you like. Jesus' manger was probably a food trough for animals. Make the manger four to six inches long.

3. **Add straw.** Press some straw or raffia into the wet clay. Arrange it evenly. Let some of the straw hang over the edges all around the manger. This straw will dry into the clay permanently. You can add more straw loosely in the manger after everything dries.

4. **Roll-up the Advent Readings.** Cut apart the Bible verses on pages 38 and 39. Roll up each one and tie it with a piece of ribbon or string. Put the readings into a resealable bag to take home. When the project is dry, tuck the readings in among the loose straw. Pull out one reading each day and read it together. Advent begins the fourth Sunday before Christmas. The number of days in Advent varies from year to year, so you may not unroll all the verses. Read any remaining verses on Christmas day.

> **Family Connections**
> - Kids learn about Advent.
> - Kids hear key Bible passages about Jesus' coming.
> - Families create a keepsake they can use every year.
> - Families read and talk about Bible verses together.

5. **Clean up.** There's plenty of work for everyone! Set the projects aside to dry until it's time to go home.

6. **Gather your group together.** Enjoy the Take It Home time together.

Take It Home

> **Bible Verse:** "The Word became flesh and made his dwelling among us. We have seen his glory, the glory of the One and Only, who came from the Father, full of grace and truth" (John 1:14).

If you have a small tent, kids will enjoy seeing it assembled. Or you can have kids help you make a tent with chairs and blankets.

How many of you have ever stayed in a tent? Pause for responses. Younger kids will be eager to tell you about their experiences. Parents may have some camping horror stories! Let people share, then ask: **What is a tent for?** A tent is shelter, protection from the weather, a place to live. Explain that nowadays we use tents for temporary shelter, but in Bible times some people lived in tents. In the Old Testament, the people had a special tent for the presence of God.

Ask a volunteer to read John 1:14 aloud. Ask: **What do you think it means that the Word became flesh?** Jesus became human. Ask: **What does it mean that He made His dwelling among us?** He came to live among us, as one of us.

Jesus was God! He came from Heaven. When He came to earth, He became human and set up His tent right next to ours. He was still God, but now He was human too. When Jesus came, He showed us the glory of God, because He was full of the glory of God himself.

Ask: **What does it mean when we say something is the "one and only"?** There isn't another one like it. **There's no one else like Jesus! That's why we celebrate that He came to earth and we look forward to the day when He'll come again. In the meantime, we wait. Advent helps us remember what we're waiting for. Jesus is coming!**

Advent Readings

Delight yourself in the Lord and he will give you the desires of your heart. Commit your way to the Lord; trust in him and he will do this.
—Psalm 37:4, 5

Sing for joy to God our strength; shout aloud to the God of Jacob!
Begin the music, strike the tambourine, play the melodious harp and lyre.
—Psalm 81:1, 2

I will sing of the Lord's great love forever; with my mouth I will make your faithfulness known through all generations. I will declare that your love stands firm forever, that you established your faithfulness in heaven itself.
—Psalm 89:1, 2

I know that my Redeemer lives, and that in the end he will stand upon the earth.
—Job 19:25

Therefore the Lord himself will give you a sign: The virgin will be with child and will give birth to a son, and will call him Immanuel.
—Isaiah 7:14

The people walking in darkness have seen a great light; on those living in the land of the shadow of death a light has dawned.
—Isaiah 9:2

For to us a child is born, to us a son is given, and the government will be on his shoulders. And he will be called Wonderful Counselor, Mighty God, Everlasting Father, Prince of Peace.
—Isaiah 9:6

A shoot will come up from the stump of Jesse; from his roots a Branch will bear fruit. The Spirit of the Lord will rest on him—the Spirit of wisdom and of understanding, the Spirit of counsel and of power, the Spirit of knowledge and of the fear of the Lord.
—Isaiah 11:1, 2

The wolf will live with the lamb, the leopard will lie down with the goat, the calf and the lion and the yearling together; and a little child will lead them.
—Isaiah 11:6

Comfort, comfort my people, says your God. Speak tenderly to Jerusalem, and proclaim to her that her hard service has been completed, that her sin has been paid for, that she has received from the Lord's hand double for all her sins. —Isaiah 40:1, 2

A voice of one calling: "In the desert prepare the way for the Lord; make straight in the wilderness a highway for our God."
—Isaiah 40:3

And the glory of the Lord will be revealed, and all mankind together will see it. For the mouth of the Lord has spoken.
—Isaiah 40:5

You who bring good tidings to Zion, go up on a high mountain. You who bring good tidings to Jerusalem, lift up your voice with a shout, lift it up, do not be afraid; say to the towns of Judah, "Here is your God!"
—Isaiah 40:9

He tends his flock like a shepherd: He gathers the lambs in his arms and carries them close to his heart; he gently leads those that have young.
—Isaiah 40:11

"Forget the former things; do not dwell on the past. See, I am doing a new thing! Now it springs up; do you not perceive it? I am making a way in the desert and streams in the wasteland."
—Isaiah 43:18, 19

How beautiful on the mountains are the feet of those who bring good news, who proclaim peace, who bring good tidings, who proclaim salvation, who say to Zion, "Your God reigns!"
—Isaiah 52:7

The Spirit of the Sovereign Lord is on me, because the Lord has anointed me to preach good news to the poor. He has sent me to bind up the brokenhearted, to proclaim freedom for the captives and release from darkness for the prisoners. —Isaiah 61:1

"For I know the plans I have for you," declares the Lord, "plans to prosper you and not to harm you, plans to give you hope and a future."
—Jeremiah 29:11

He will stand and shepherd his flock in the strength of the Lord, in the majesty of the name of the Lord his God. And they will live securely, for then his greatness will reach to the ends of the earth.
—Micah 5:4

"Come to me, all you who are weary and burdened, and I will give you rest. Take my yoke upon you and learn from me, for I am gentle and humble in heart, and you will find rest for your souls. For my yoke is easy and my burden is light." —Matthew 11:28-30

In the beginning was the Word, and the Word was with God, and the Word was God. He was with God in the beginning.
—John 1:1, 2

The light shines in the darkness, but the darkness has not understood it.
—John 1:5

For God so loved the world that he gave his one and only Son, that whoever believes in him shall not perish but have eternal life. For God did not send his Son into the world to condemn the world, but to save the world through him.
—John 3:16, 17

And how can they preach unless they are sent? As it is written, "How beautiful are the feet of those who bring good news!"
—Romans 10:15

May our Lord Jesus Christ himself and God our Father, who loved us and by his grace gave us eternal encouragement and good hope, encourage your hearts and strengthen you in every good deed and word.
—2 Thessalonians 2:16, 17

How great is the love the Father has lavished on us, that we should be called children of God! And that is what we are!
—1 John 3:1

Then I heard what sounded like a great multitude, like the roar of rushing waters and like loud peals of thunder, shouting: "Hallelujah! For our Lord God Almighty reigns."
—Revelation 19:6

"The kingdom of the world has become the kingdom of our Lord and of his Christ, and he will reign for ever and ever."
—Revelation 11:15

Copyright © 2007 by Susan Martins Miller. Permission is granted to reproduce this page for ministry purposes only—not for resale.

Cozy Cards

Everybody loves to get a card. It's such a lift to know that someone else is thinking of you and took the time to express care. Use these Cozy Cards to help families express their care for others in a variety of situations.

Set It Up

Supplies:

- colorful card stock
- scissors
- glue
- markers
- copies of Stencil Card on page 42
- copies of Pop-up Card on page 43
- paintbrushes
- poster paints
- markers
- waxed paper
- water for clean up

Optional:

- paint smocks or shirts
- craft knife

Do Ahead ≫ Photocopy pages 42 and 43 on colorful card stock. Tear off strips of waxed paper about 12″ x 18″.

Option! ≫ Some of the more creative participants might enjoy making their own stencil shapes.

Get It Done ≫ 1. **Choose a card.** Choose a copy of page 42 or 43 and cut apart the card on the bottom half of the page. Cut out the stencils or pop-up banners on the top half. Use a sheet of waxed paper as a working surface.

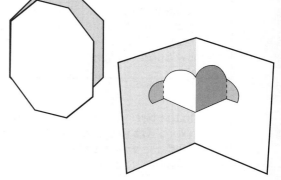

2. **Write your message.** You can make a get-well card, a birthday card, a friendship card, an encouragement card, or any other kind of card you'd like. Decide how you want to use your card and write a message. If you are making a stencil card, write the message inside the card. If you are making a pop-up card, write the message on the pop-up shape you chose.

3. **Stencil.** If you're making a stencil card, cut apart the squares of stencil shapes. Then cut out the center shape without cutting through to the edge of the square. You may want to use a craft knife rather than scissors. Make sure children are supervised. Position a shape on the front of the card and hold it in place with one hand. Use paint or marker to color the inside of the stencil shape. Use as many shapes as you like to make a design.

4. **Make a pop-up.** If you're making a pop-up card, cut out the pop-up shape you've selected. Fold the side tabs forward and crease. Line up the center of the pop-up with the center crease of the card. Make sure the pop-up is not flat but arches over the card. Glue the pop-up into the inside of the card at the tabs only. When you close the card, the pop-up will fold too. When you open the card, the message pops up.

5. **Plan your delivery.** Choose a time when you can deliver your card to the person for whom you made it.

6. **Make an envelope.** (Optional) Use plain card stock to make envelopes. Glue two pieces of card stock together along three edges. Leave the fourth edge open. Make sure the card is dry before you put it in the envelope.

7. **Clean up.** There's plenty of work for everyone. Give younger kids specific tasks to help them feel valued.

8. **Gather your group together.** Enjoy the Take It Home time together.

> ## Family Connections
>
> - Kids and parents talk about people they care about.
> - Kids learn a new method of card-making they can use again at home.
> - Parents have an opportunity to encourage kids to express care for others in tangible ways.

Take It Home 〉 **Bible Verse:** "A friend loves at all times" (Proverbs 17:17).

Ahead of time, write the letters of the word *encourage* on index cards, one letter per card. Mix up the cards. When the group gathers, shuffle the cards around and say: **I've got an important word in here somewhere. I'm just not sure what it is. I'm going to need some help.** Lay out the cards so you can see them all. Choose some volunteers to help you put them in the right order.

Say: **Encourage! That's it. That's my important word.** Ask participants to tell you about the greeting cards they made and how they plan to use them. As a visual aid, you may want to make a list of the variety of cards on a board or newsprint pad.

We made cards to show people that we care about them. We wrote messages inside the cards to let them know we're thinking about them. Look at all the different kinds of cards we made!

The Bible tells us that "A friend loves at all times." Ask kids and parents to tell you about times that someone expressed love for them, especially in tough times. Encourage parents to speak up. It's great for kids to hear parents talk about their spiritual journeys and other topics that may not come up at home.

A card seems like a simple thing, but it can be a great encouragement and a great expression of love. Cards remind us that we can care for each other in simple ways. The next time you send a card, pray for the recipient.

Copyright © 2007 by Susan Martins Miller. Permission is granted to reproduce this page for ministry purposes only—not for resale.

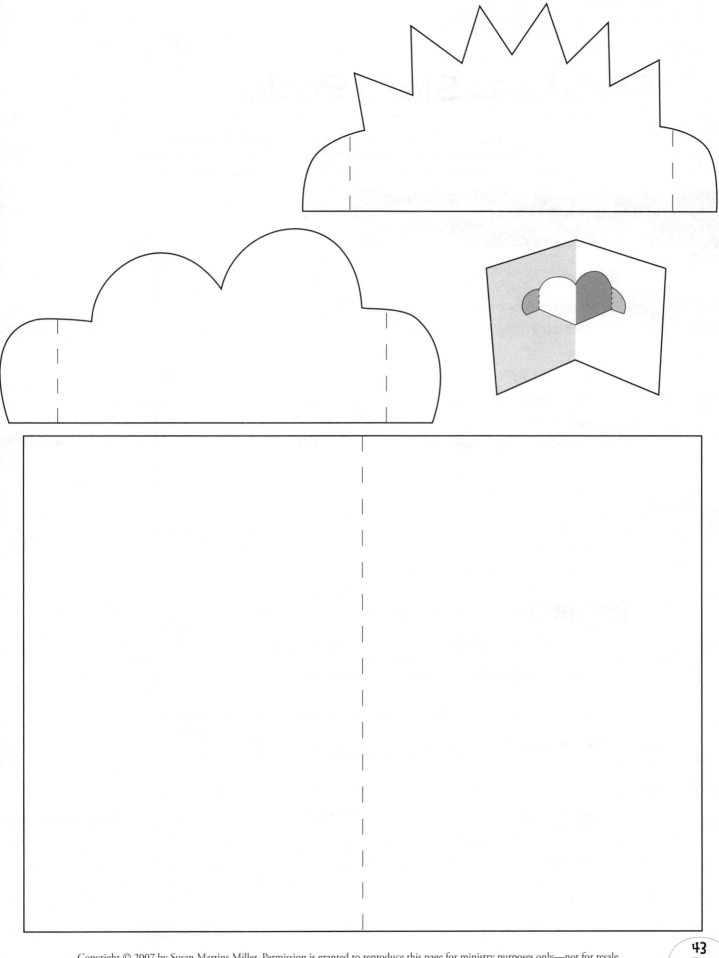

Copyright © 2007 by Susan Martins Miller. Permission is granted to reproduce this page for ministry purposes only—not for resale.

Christmas Story Books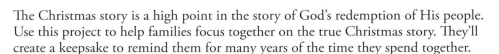

The Christmas story is a high point in the story of God's redemption of His people. Use this project to help families focus together on the true Christmas story. They'll create a keepsake to remind them for many years of the time they spend together.

Set It Up

Supplies:

- manila folders
- card stock
- glue
- Christmas wrapping paper
- clear adhesive covering
- old Christmas cards
- copies of Christmas Story on page 46
- scissors
- colored wide electrician's tape

Optional:

- crayons or markers

Do Ahead >> If time for your session is limited, you may want to cut manila folders and card stock to uniform sizes ahead of time. These will become the book cover and pages. Also cut pieces of clear adhesive covering slightly larger than the size you choose for the book pages. If you have time during your session, families may choose their own sizes and cut pages themselves. Hint: You won't waste paper if you choose to cut your sheets in half or quarters.

Option! >> Ask families to bring old Christmas cards to mix and share.

Get It Done >> 1. **Cut book cover and pages.** Choose the size that you want your book to be. Cut the two halves of a manila folder to that size. Then cut card stock to the same size. Plan on six card stock pages for your book.

2. **Make the cover.** Cut a piece of Christmas wrapping paper to match the size of your book cover. Glue it to the cover and trim. Then cut a piece of clear self-adhesive covering slightly larger than the cover. Lay the paper in front of you sticky side up and peel off the paper backing. Put your book cover face down on the self-adhesive covering and smooth in place. Fold the edges of the self-adhesive covering over the edges of your book cover. Repeat for the back cover of your book.

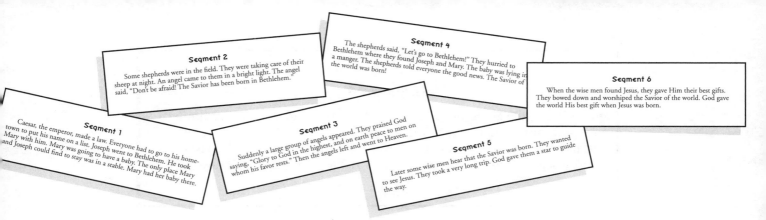

Segment 1
Caesar, the emperor, made a law. Everyone had to go to his hometown to put his name on a list. Joseph went to Bethlehem. He took Mary with him. Mary was going to have a baby. The only place Mary and Joseph could find to stay was in a stable. Mary had her baby there.

Segment 2
Some shepherds were in the field. They were taking care of their sheep at night. An angel came to them in a bright light. The angel said, "Don't be afraid! The Savior has been born in Bethlehem."

Segment 3
Suddenly a large group of angels appeared. They praised God saying, "Glory to God in the highest, and on earth peace to men on whom his favor rests." Then the angels left and went to Heaven.

Segment 4
The shepherds said, "Let's go to Bethlehem!" They hurried to Bethlehem where they found Joseph and Mary. The baby was lying in a manger. The shepherds told everyone the good news. The Savior of the world was born!

Segment 5
Later some wise men hear that the Savior was born. They wanted to see Jesus. They took a very long trip. God gave them a star to guide the way.

Segment 6
When the wise men found Jesus, they gave Him their best gifts. They bowed down and worshiped the Savior of the world. God gave the world His best gift when Jesus was born.

3. **Make the book pages.** Cut apart the story strips from the handout. Look for pictures on old Christmas cards to match the words of the story segments. Arrange a story strip and matching picture on a page in a way that you think looks nice. Draw pictures if you can't find illustrations to match.

4. **Bind the book.** Stack the pages in order between the book covers. Have one person hold the stack together tightly. Have someone else measure a piece of wide colorful tape the same length as the side of the book. Wrap the book in the tape to bind it. Then carefully open the book and put a small amount of glue on each page close to the binding and press the pages together. Take turns holding the book tightly until the glue dries.

5. **Clean up.** Send kids around with trash bags for paper scraps. Collect supplies.

6. **Gather your group together.** Enjoy the Take It Home time together.

Family Connections

- Families create a lasting memory they can share in the future.
- Families pause during a busy season to celebrate the true meaning of Christmas.
- Parents have an opportunity to talk about other family Christmas traditions with their kids.

Take It Home

Bible Verse: "Glory to God in the highest, and on earth peace to men on whom his favor rests" (Luke 2:14).

Encourage families to share the books they have made with other families in your group. Ask participants to show their favorite pictures or talk about their favorite parts of the Christmas story.

Hold up some of the leftover Christmas cards. **How many of you received a Christmas card this year?** Pause. **How many of you are sending Christmas cards this year?** Pause.

Have you ever wondered about the first Christmas card? Before Christmas cards, people used to visit each other in person to exchange holiday greetings. Then they began sending handmade cards. In 1843, people could buy printed Christmas cards for the first time. Now many companies print Christmas cards. But it's still nice to get a homemade one!

We still use Christmas cards to send greetings to our friends and family. This is one way that we celebrate the story of Christmas. When you get a card with a picture of shepherds or angels or baby Jesus in the manger, you remember the whole story.

Choose a volunteer to read Luke 2:14 aloud for the group. Ask: **Why do we use this verse to celebrate Christmas?** It's what the angels said to the shepherds and reminds us the glory of God that came to earth when Jesus was born. **Let's read the Christmas story together.** Have families or individuals gather around their books as the whole group reads the story together.

Segment 1 ▶

Caesar, the emperor, made a law. Everyone had to go to his hometown to put his name on a list. Joseph went to Bethlehem. He took Mary with him. Mary was going to have a baby. The only place Mary and Joseph could find to stay was in a stable. Mary had her baby there.

Segment 2 ▶

Some shepherds were in the field. They were taking care of their sheep at night. An angel came to them in a bright light. The angel said, "Don't be afraid! The Savior has been born in Bethlehem."

Segment 3 ▶

Suddenly a large group of angels appeared. They praised God saying, "Glory to God in the highest, and on earth peace to men on whom his favor rests." Then the angels left and went to Heaven.

Segment 4 ▶

The shepherds said, "Let's go to Bethlehem!" They hurried to Bethlehem where they found Joseph and Mary. The baby was lying in a manger. The shepherds told everyone the good news. The Savior of the world was born!

Segment 5 ▶

Later some wise men hear that the Savior was born. They wanted to see Jesus. They took a very long trip. God gave them a star to guide the way.

Segment 6 ▶

When the wise men found Jesus, they gave Him their best gifts. They bowed down and worshiped the Savior of the world. God gave the world His best gift when Jesus was born.

Copyright © 2007 by Susan Martins Miller. Permission is granted to reproduce this page for ministry purposes only—not for resale.

International Intrigue

The world has gotten a lot smaller. We can e-mail the other side of the world and get an answer in seconds, when it used to take weeks to send letters back and forth. Use this event to help families in your congregation think about sharing Jesus with people in other countries.

Set It Up

Supplies:

- maps or globes
- copies of International Intrigue Instructions on page 49
- index cards or construction paper in four colors
- Bibles
- bowl of honey
- plastic spoons
- 4 baskets or small boxes
- flashlight
- food, clothing, household items, or other decorations to represent various continents or cultures
- megaphone
- keyboard

Do Ahead ▷ Collect items to decorate four continent stations in various parts of a large room or in separate rooms in the church building: Europe, Latin America, Africa, and Asia. Try to have a map at each station that highlights that continent. Ask members of your congregation to contribute international items and gather as many as you can to decorate each station.

Option! ▷ Ask others to prepare food that represents various cultures and encourage people to try a bite at each station.

Get It Done ▷ 1. **Set up stations.** Make copies of International Intrigue Instructions on page 49. Cut apart the four cards and place one at each station along with a Bible. Participants will follow the instruction card to read a Bible verse and respond. At the station with Psalm 34:8, place

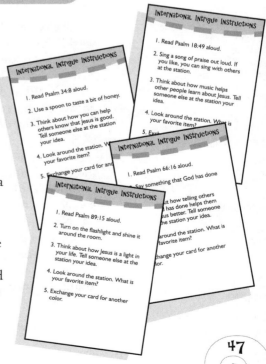

International Intrigue Instructions

1. Read Psalm 18:49 aloud.
2. Sing a song of praise out loud. If you like, you can sing with others at the station.
3. Think about how music helps other people learn about Jesus. Tell someone else at the station your idea.
4. Look around the station. What is your favorite item?
5. Exc...

International Intrigue Instructions

1. Read Psalm 34:8 aloud.
2. Use a spoon to taste a bit of honey.
3. Think about how you can help others know that Jesus is good. Tell someone else at the station your idea.
4. Look around the station. W... your favorite item?
5. Exchange your card for and...

International Intrigue Instructions

1. Read Psalm 66:16 aloud.
2. Say something that God has done ...
...ut how telling others ...has done helps them ...us better. Tell someone ...he station your idea.
...around the station. What is ...favorite item?
...change your card for another ...or.

International Intrigue Instructions

1. Read Psalm 89:15 aloud.
2. Turn on the flashlight and shine it around the room.
3. Think about how Jesus is a light in your life. Tell someone else at the station your idea.
4. Look around the station. What is your favorite item?
5. Exchange your card for another color.

a bowl of honey and plastic spoons. At the station with Psalm 89:15, place a flashlight. At the station with Psalm 66:16, place a megaphone, and at the station with Psalm 18:49, place a keyboard or set up the station in a room with a piano.

2. **Assign colors.** Assign one of the four colors of index cards or construction paper to each station and tape a sample to the wall in a prominent location. If you'd like, you can label each index card with the name of a continent. Make sure you use only one color for each continent. Put an extra supply of extra cards in a bowl or basket at each station, but leave out the color for that station. Put enough cards in each basket for everyone who participates.

3. **Distribute cards.** Give everyone an index card (or quartered construction paper). Mix up the colors. Older kids might want to explore independently with their own cards. Parents can pair up with younger kids to visit the stations together.

4. **Exchange cards.** Explain that each participant should go to the station represented by the card she is holding in her hand. When she gets there, she'll find the International Intrigue Instructions. Each person should follow the instructions on the card. When each person has finished, ask her to put her colored card in the basket or box and take a new colored card. Then she goes to the station represented by that card and follows the instructions. Keep going until each person has visited every station.

5. **Assemble**. When they've been to all four stations, have participants return to the main area. Ask them to bring the last colored cards they used. This should be a different card than the one with which they started.

6. **Gather your group together.** Enjoy the Take It Home time together.

Family Connections

- Kids and parents share in reading the Bible.
- Parents and younger kids worship and pray together.
- Families have a starting point for talking about missions at home.

Take It Home

> **Bible Verse:** "Therefore go and make disciples of all nations, baptizing them in the name of the Father and of the Son and of the Holy Spirit" (Matthew 28:19).

We've been all over the world together. What's your favorite part of the world? Pause for responses.

Did you know Jesus told us to go all over the world? Ask a volunteer to read Matthew 28:19 from a Bible.

Ask: **What do you think it means to make disciples?** Kids and parents will answer on different levels, so encourage participation from all age groups.

Ask: **Why does Jesus tell us to go to all nations?** God loves everyone in the world and wants everyone to know the good news.

Ask those who have a North American card to raise their hands. Repeat with the other continents. Then ask participants to regroup by finding people with other continent cards. A complete group will have all four cards regardless of how many people join the group.

Now you're a mixed-up bunch! Having the various continents together in one group reminds us that in many ways the world has gotten smaller. We can visit other countries more easily than in the past and communicate with people in those countries more easily. The next time you look at a map or eat food from another country, remember that Jesus wants the whole world to know Him.

International Intrigue Instructions

1. Read Psalm 34:8 aloud.

2. Use a spoon to taste a bit of honey.

3. Think about how you can help others know that Jesus is good. Tell someone else at the station your idea.

4. Look around the station. What is your favorite item?

5. Exchange your card for another color.

International Intrigue Instructions

1. Read Psalm 18:49 aloud.

2. Sing a song of praise out loud. If you like, you can sing with others at the station.

3. Think about how music helps other people learn about Jesus. Tell someone else at the station your idea.

4. Look around the station. What is your favorite item?

5. Exchange your card for another color.

International Intrigue Instructions

1. Read Psalm 66:16 aloud.

2. Say something that God has done for you.

3. Think about how telling others what God has done helps them know Jesus better. Tell someone else at the station your idea.

4. Look around the station. What is your favorite item?

5. Exchange your card for another color.

International Intrigue Instructions

1. Read Psalm 89:15 aloud.

2. Turn on the flashlight and shine it around the room.

3. Think about how Jesus is a light in your life. Tell someone else at the station your idea.

4. Look around the station. What is your favorite item?

5. Exchange your card for another color.

Copyright © 2007 by Susan Martins Miller. Permission is granted to reproduce this page for ministry purposes only—not for resale.

How Many Ways Can You Pray?

"Close your eyes and fold your hands," we tell small children when we teach them to pray. Children do need to learn to quiet themselves before God. As they grow older, though, we can help them expand the concept of prayer in ways that touch personalities and individuality.

Set It Up

Supplies:

- Bibles
- copies of Prayer Stations instructions on pages 52 and 53
- tables
- paper
- pens
- beads or buttons
- bowls
- poster board
- markers

Do Ahead ≫ Photocopy the Prayer Stations instructions and set up four stations with supplies. Follow the set-up instructions below. These can be in four sections of one large room or in four separate rooms that families can visit. Some stations require more quiet than others.

Option! ≫ Have families who arrive early work together to set up a station.

Get It Done ≫ 1. **Set up Station 1.** On a table set out a selection of colored markers and poster board. Families will choose a faith word and write an acrostic poem to take home. Set out one or more copies of the Pray Acrostic instructions.

2. **Set up Station 2.** Set out several Bibles. Put bookmarks at the suggested references. Label the bookmarks clearly at the top so people who may not be familiar with the Bible can find the passages easily. You may even want to highlight the verses. Set out one or more copies of the Pray Scripture instructions.

3. **Set up Station 3.** Set out bowls with about 50 beads or buttons in each. Also set out one empty bowl per family to transfer beads to as they count their blessings. Set out one or more copies of Count Your Blessings instructions.

4. **Set up Station 4.** Set out paper and pens or pencils and have some Bibles handy. Set out one or more copies of Family Prayer instructions.

5. **Invite families to choose a prayer station.** Explain the main activity at each station. Families have the opportunity to go to several, or all, of the prayer stations, depending on the time available or how long they spend at each station. At each station, have families read the instructions and follow them together. It's OK if they don't get to every station.

6. **Gather your group together.** Enjoy the Take It Home time together.

Family Connections

- Kids and parents pray together.
- Families learn methods they can use together at home.
- Kids see a devotional side of parents.
- Parents have the opportunity to be positive models.

Take It Home

> **Bible Verse:** "Be joyful always; pray continually; give thanks in all circumstances, for this is God's will for you in Christ Jesus" (1 Thessalonians 5:16-18).

How many of you are wearing a watch? Take off your watch and hold it up. Pause for responses. Ask: **What do we use watches for?** Kids will probably answer that watches tell us what time it is. Adults may give more complex answers that watches tell us how long something takes or help us be on time.

Ask: **Do you ever wish you could do something all the time?** Pause for answers.

Our Bible verses have some words about doing things at all times. Ask a volunteer to read 1 Thessalonians 5:16-18. Ask: **What *time* words did you hear?** (always, continually, in all circumstances)

Ask: **What should we be doing all the time?** (be joyful, pray, give thanks) **Always is a long time. Let's see if we can be joyful for 30 seconds. Do something that shows you're joyful, and I'll let you know when time is up. Ready?** Go. Call time after 30 seconds.

Thirty seconds seems like a long time when you're thinking about it and watching the second hand tick. But what if I asked you to breathe for 30 seconds? Would that be hard? No, breathing comes naturally. We don't have to think about it.

God didn't say he wants us to *think* about being joyful and praying all the time. He wants us to *be* joyful, *be* prayerful, and *be* thankful all the time—naturally.

Everybody take a deep breath, and when you let it out, think a prayer in your head.

Pray Acrostic

An acrostic poem uses the letters in a word. Each line in the poem starts with a letter in the word. For example:

J Jesus loves us.
O Our hope is in God.
Y You are my strength.

Choose one of the following words and write an acrostic poem prayer together as a family: trust, hope, thanks, or faith. Write the letters of the word down the left side of a piece of poster board. Then write about things you want to pray for. Start each line with the next letter in the word.

T **H** **T** **F**
R **O** **H** **A**
U **P** **A** **I**
S **E** **N** **T**
T   **K** **H**
           S

Pray Scripture

The Bible tells us to pray, and it also shows us how to pray. People in the Bible prayed for help, for forgiveness, for trust, and for protection. They prayed with thanksgiving and praise and joy.

Choose several prayers from the Bible to read together as a family. Then talk about one thing you can learn about prayer from each example.

If your children are very young, choose from these sentence prayers.

A Prayer for Renewal	Psalm 51:10
A Prayer for Protection	Psalm 86:1
A Prayer for Joy	Psalm 86:4, 5
A Prayer of Praise	Psalm 103:1, 2
A Prayer for Direction	2 Thessalonians 3:5

If your children are older, choose from these longer prayers.

A Prayer for Guidance	Psalm 25:1-7
David's Prayer for Forgiveness	Psalm 51:1-13
Mary's Prayer	Luke 1:46-55
The Lord's Prayer	Luke 11:2-4
Paul's Prayer for the Ephesians	Ephesians 3:14-19
Paul's Prayer for the Colossians	Colossians 1:3-6

Copyright © 2007 by Susan Martins Miller. Permission is granted to reproduce this page for ministry purposes only—not for resale.

Count Your Blessings

God loves it when we're thankful! But sometimes we don't appreciate how much God gives us. If we don't have everything we want, we may not be thankful for what we do have.

Count your family blessings. Sit in a circle with a bowl of beads or buttons and an empty bowl in the circle. Take turns moving a bead or button to the empty bowl. With each bead, name one blessing that God has given your family. Can you count enough blessings to move all the beads or buttons to the empty bowl?

Family Prayer

Write a prayer that can become special to your family. Start by choosing a theme:

praise
thankfulness
joy
trust
hope

Decide on a sentence that you can say together after each prayer. This can be anything you want it to be. It can be as simple as, "Lord, hear our prayer." Or you can use the words from a favorite Bible verse.

Then write brief sentences that tell God how you feel. Take turns deciding what the next sentence should be. After each sentence, say your response together.

If you'd like, you can write a rough draft and copy a clean version on fresh paper to take home. Talk about times that you can use this prayer together at home.

Copyright © 2007 by Susan Martins Miller. Permission is granted to reproduce this page for ministry purposes only—not for resale.

God of Wonders Science

When it comes to how our bodies work or how the world around us works, we take a lot of things for granted. Understanding science may help us understand why things happen the way they do, but science can never explain the God who is behind everything that happens. Use these demonstrations to inspire awe and wonder in your families.

Set It Up

Supplies:

- copies of Super Science on pages 56 and 57
- large resealable bag
- sharpened pencil
- plastic cups
- water
- tissues
- pebbles
- balloons
- empty, clean soda bottles
- baking soda
- juice from one lemon
- straw
- tables
- volunteers for each station
- Bibles
- timer or bell

Optional:

- masking tape

Do Ahead ⟩ Set up the supplies at each station. Use as many stations as you'd like. These can all be in one large room. Arrange for volunteers to do the demonstrations at each station and give them an opportunity to try the demonstrations ahead of time so they're confident in doing them.

Option! ⟩ Add some other science demonstrations you think are cool.

Get It Done

1. **Meet with station volunteers.** Gather your volunteers ahead of time and explain how God of Wonders Science will work. Several families at a time will visit each science station. Encourage station volunteers to let kids participate in a hands-on way with the demonstrations. It's OK if kids want to repeat a demonstration.

2. **Clarify instructions.** Make sure volunteers understand how to do each demonstration. If you have time, you may want to do all four demonstrations for your group of volunteers. If you expect a large group, you may want to set up duplicate stations or add more demonstrations. Try to keep the number of people at each station small enough that everyone can see and participate.

3. **Make a faith connection.** Ask the volunteers to read the Bible verses listed under What You Learn after each demonstration or ask a participant to read them from a Bible. Using the suggestion on the instruction card, make a brief faith connection between the demonstration and the verse. Volunteers who are comfortable doing so may expand or facilitate a brief discussion with families.

> ## Family Connections
> - Kids and parents share a hands-on experience.
> - Kids and parents learn together.
> - Families celebrate our amazing God.

4. **Invite families to visit stations.** When families have gathered, encourage them to experience the awe and wonder of God's creation! Point out where the stations are and let families know they may move to a new station every 10 minutes or so. Use a timer or bell, or make an announcement, when it's time to rotate between stations.

5. **Gather your group together.** Enjoy the Take It Home time together.

Take It Home

Bible Verse: "Praise the Lord. Praise God in his sanctuary; praise him in his mighty heavens. Praise him for his acts of power; praise him for his surpassing greatness. Praise him with the sounding of the trumpet, praise him with the harp and lyre, praise him with tambourine and dancing, praise him with the strings and flute, praise him with the clash of cymbals, praise him with resounding symbols. Let everything that has breath praise the Lord. Praise the Lord" (Psalm 150).

Ahead of time, gather enough Bibles for each reader to have one, or make photocopies of Psalm 150.

Raise your hand if you learned something new at one of the science stations. A lot of hands should go up! **Raise your hand if you think what you saw was cool.** Pause.

God is amazing! Scientists work hard to try to understand the world, but God is the one who thought of it all in the first place! I have a feeling God will keep surprising scientists for a very long time. Let's praise our amazing God.

Distribute Bibles or copies of Psalm 150. Point out how this short psalm is made up of simple phrases that all begin with the word *praise.* Have one person read the first phrase and another person read the second phrase. Then anyone can repeat the first two phrases, or add the third phrase. After that, anyone can repeat the first three phrases, or add the fourth phrase. Keep going until all the phrases have been introduced. If you think it would be easier for your group, don't worry about the order at all. Anyone can read any phrase at any time. Enjoy a time of pop-up praise, and then end in unison with the last verse: Let everything that has breath praise the Lord. Praise the Lord.

Trust Bag

What You Need: resealable bag full of water, sharpened pencil
Optional: basin or sink

What You Do: Hold the bag of water over someone's head. Look for a bulge in the bag that has no wrinkles. Use a twisting motion and push the sharpened pencil point into the bag until you break the surface. It shouldn't leak! Keep twisting until the pencil pokes out the other side of the bag. Don't pull the pencil out until you're ready to drain the bag!

What You Learn: Who do you trust? God never lets you down. You can always depend on him. "Some trust in chariots and some in horses, but we trust in the name of the Lord our God" (Psalm 20:7).

Fun Fact: The bag is made of polymer, a chemical compound. When you poke a hole in the bag, the plastic closes around the pencil, sealing it closed.

Soppy Rocks

What You Need: plastic cups, water, tissues, rubber bands, pebbles

What You Do: Lay a tissue over an empty plastic cup. Use the rubber band to hold the tissue around the rim of the cup. Dip your fingers in water and drop four or five drops of water onto the tissue. Gently add pebbles to the tissue to see how many it will hold. (Depending on the strength of the tissue, it will hold 7–12 small stones. Two layers will hold more.)

What You Learn: What do you put your confidence in? We can always be sure that God is on our side. "For you have been my hope, O Sovereign Lord, my confidence since my youth" (Psalm 71:5).

Copyright © 2007 by Susan Martins Miller. Permission is granted to reproduce this page for ministry purposes only—not for resale.

Walls of Tension

What You Need: walls

Optional: masking tape to mark a line three inches from the wall

What You Do: Face a wall with your toes about three inches from the wall with arms down in front of you. Press the backs of your wrists to the wall. Count slowly to 30. Then step back from the wall. When you release the muscle tension, your arms will seem to float up.

What You Learn: We suffer a lot of tension that we don't need to go through. Take your concerns to God in prayer. He never gets stressed out! "Do not be anxious about anything, but in everything, by prayer and petition, with thanksgiving, present your requests to God" (Philippians 4:6).

Baking Soda Balloon

What You Need: balloons; empty, clean soda bottles; water; baking soda; juice from one lemon; straw

What You Do: Fill the bottle one-quarter full of water. Sprinkle 1 tsp. of baking soda into the bottle and use the straw to stir it. Add the lemon juice. Quickly stretch an uninflated balloon over the mouth of the bottle. The balloon inflates!

What You Learn: Faith is being sure of what we can't see. We can't see what inflates the balloon, but we know it's there. We can't see faith, but we know it's there. "Now faith is being sure of what we hope for and certain of what we do not see" (Hebrews 11:1).

Fun Fact: Baking soda is a base and lemon juice is an acid. When a base and acid come together, the reaction forms carbon dioxide gas. As the gas rises, it inflates the balloon.

Copyright © 2007 by Susan Martins Miller. Permission is granted to reproduce this page for ministry purposes only—not for resale.

What's Mine Is Yours: Book and Toy Swap

It's easy to accumulate a lot of stuff! Sometimes it's hard to get rid of it. We know someone could use it, and we feel better if we know our items are going to a good home. The book and toy swap gives families an opportunity to be grateful for God's abundance to them by sharing with others.

Set It Up

Supplies:

- copies of Tag It! on page 60
- markers
- clear tape
- scissors
- tables
- Bible

Optional:

- signs to help sort donated items
- large boxes for leftover items
- snacks

Do Ahead ≫ Invite families and individuals to bring various books and toys for all ages to swap. Encourage adults to bring contributions as well as the kids. These could be books, toys or baby items kids have outgrown but a younger family might want, cookbooks you don't use, novels you've read several times, discipleship books that have touched your life. Emphasize that items should be in good condition. Families should try to bring at least one item per person, but they can bring as many as they want.

Option! ≫ Have early arrivers help cut out tags from the reproducible page.

Get It Done ≫ 1. **Photocopy Tag It!** on page 60. Make copies on several bright colors of paper. Cut them out ahead of time or leave copies out for families to cut together.

2. **Set up tables.** Set up several tables in a large room on which to put donations. If you prefer, make signs that describe various categories and hang them on or above tables. When participants arrive, have them place their items on the appropriate tables. For instance, categories might help sort toys by age group or type of book. Also set up one or more tables on which to set tags, markers, and tape.

3. **Write tags.** As you welcome families, direct them to tables with tags, markers, and tape. Explain that each person should fill out a tag for the item she brought and then place the item on the swap tables. Each tag will list who brought the item and why she liked it. You may have a lot of people writing tags at the beginning, so make sure to have enough space for this.

4. **Swap!** Allow time for adults and kids to walk around and see what's on the tables. They may choose to take home as many items as they brought. If it looks like you have plenty of items, let people choose more than one. Try to make sure no one goes home empty-handed unless they want to. Explain: **When you find something you'd like to take home, find the person who wrote the tag. Tell that person why you chose that item. Ask the person to tell you a memory about the item.**

5. **Gather your group together.** Enjoy the Take It Home time together.

6. **Box up the leftovers.** Make sure people understand they don't have to take home items they brought that were not selected. Make arrangements to donate leftover items to a community organization, such as a school or library, tutoring program, adult literacy program, or thrift store. Individual families may enjoy making the donations together as a family service project.

Family Connections

- Kids see parents being generous.
- Families celebrate the way they have grown over the years.
- Families connect with other families, possibly to begin new friendships.
- Sharing is a model of stewardship of God's gifts.

Take It Home

> **Bible Verse:** "All the believers were one in heart and mind. No one claimed that any of his possessions was his own, but they shared everything they had" (Acts 4:32).

As participants gather, ask them to share about the items they selected. Then ask: **Tell me how you felt when you found something you wanted to take home.** Pause for responses. **Now tell me how you felt when someone chose an item that you brought.** Pause for responses.

We feel good when we know that something we don't need anymore will make someone else happy. Everything we have comes from God. We please God when we share with other people what He gives to us.

Ask a volunteer to read Acts 4:32 from a Bible. Ask: **What do you think it means to be one in heart and mind?** Make sure kids get a chance to answer, even if it seems like a hard question for them. The early believers didn't think just about themselves, but about what others needed as well.

Ask: **What's the hardest thing you ever had to share?** Pause for responses. Try to get answers from people of various ages. **Sharing doesn't always come easy. Sometimes we want to hang on to things long after we need them. But think of how good it feels when you know you've made someone happy because you gave him something he needed.**

Close with prayer thanking God for His blessings and asking for opportunities to share with others.

Tag It!

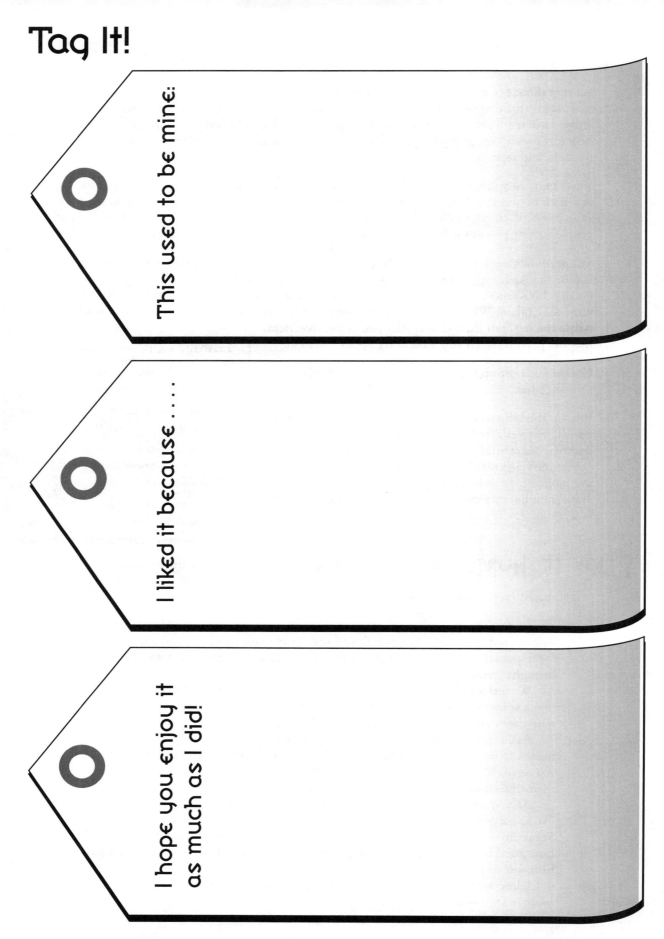

This used to be mine:

I liked it because . . . . .

I hope you enjoy it as much as I did!

Copyright © 2007 by Susan Martins Miller. Permission is granted to reproduce this page for ministry purposes only—not for resale.

Upside Down and Inside Out

Sometimes nothing seems to go right. Everybody has days when he feels jumbled up and nothing makes sense. Why not have fun with it? Use this meal to remind families and individuals that God is the one who sets them straight.

Set It Up

SUPPLIES:

- place settings
- pictures and other room accents
- extra items of clothing
- magazine pictures
- name tags
- markers
- masking tape
- Bible
- salad
- main dish
- dessert
- copy of Verse Cards on page 63
- paper lunch bag

Optional:

- appetizer

Do Ahead ≫ Let families know ahead of time to come dressed inside out and upside down. Help advertise the event by showing up at church one Sunday dressed up in a mixed-up manner. When you set up your room, turn all the pictures upside down or tape some magazine pictures on the walls upside down. Look around your room and turn anything you can upside down or inside out.

Option! ≫ Make the meal a potluck and have participants bring the food.

Get It Done

> 1. **Set up for the meal.** Keep things simple with paper plates and cups and plastic silverware. Stack plates upside down. When you set up your serving area, look for something to jumble up or set cock-eyed. If you're using tablecloths or placements, use them wrong side up or at strange angles. Let your imagination run loose looking for ways to mix things up.

2. **Welcome everyone.** As participants arrive, make sure everyone gets a name tag—to wear upside down, of course. Older elementary kids might like to be in charge of the name table, or assign the job to a family to do together. If people arrive without clothing turned inside out or upside down, encourage them to go to the restroom and switch their clothes around or give them some funny items they can wear. (Examples: plastic glasses to wear on the back of the head or ties to be worn on the back.)

3. **Celebrate being jumbled up.** Have a quick time of demonstrations or games. See who can walk on their hands or do backward somersaults. Challenge kids to a crabwalk race—on their hands and feet but facing up. See if anyone can say the alphabet backward—or the books of the New Testament. Count backward together from 100. Use any backward and upside down ideas you have.

4. **Serve the meal.** Explain that the meal is backward! Participants should go through the line walking backward. Start with dessert. (Keep portions small to save appetites for the main dishes.) Then move to the main dish and finish up with salads. Pour cold drinks from coffee pitchers. Put the wrong kind of serving utensils in the dishes.

5. **Gather your group together.** After the meal, enjoy the Take It Home time together.

Family Connections

- Kids see a silly side of their parents.
- Families laugh together!
- Kids realize even grown-ups feel confused sometimes.
- Families learn a Bible verse together.

Take It Home

> **Bible Verse:** "He lifted me out of the slimy pit, out of the mud and mire; he set my feet on a rock and gave me a firm place to stand" (Psalm 40:2).

Ahead of time, photocopy the Verse Cards on page 63 and cut them apart. Mix them up so they are not in order and put them in a paper lunch sack.

As you gather the group, find out what has been the favorite part of Upside Down and Inside Out for everyone.

Say: **Tell me about a time when you felt all jumbled up and confused.** Encourage responses from children and adults. Then ask: **What did you do about it? How did you get straightened out?** Pause for responses.

Just when we feel like our lives are upside down and inside out, God turns us right side out and sets us on our feet. Let's read a Bible verse about that. Ask a volunteer to read Psalm 40:2 from a Bible.

Ask: **Have you ever felt like your life was a slimy pit or a big mud puddle? What was that like?**

Ask: **What does it mean that God gives us a firm place to stand?**

Let's learn this Bible verse together. Read the verse once again a phrase at a time and have the group repeat after you. **I've got all the parts of this verse in this bag, but they're all jumbled up. Let's see if we can straighten them out.** Have kids come forward and draw cards out of the bag and try to place each card in correct order in relation to the others. Let kids look at a Bible if they need to. Kids can stand and hold the cards in order or tape them to the wall one at a time.

The next time you feel all upside down and inside out, remember—God is the one who straightens you out!

Optional: End your time together with an appetizer to encourage lingering fellowship.

"He lifted Me

out of the slimy pit,

out of the mud and mire;

He set my feet

on a rock

and gave me

a firm place to stand."

Psalm 40:2

Copyright © 2007 by Susan Martins Miller. Permission is granted to reproduce this page for ministry purposes only—not for resale.

Story Time

Everybody loves a good story. Stories help people connect with each other and help people remember and learn from the past. Have a congregational story time to help the people in your church build connections and share the faith story together.

Set It Up

Supplies:

* favorite children's books
* stools
* music stands
* copies of Tell Me a Story on pages 66 and 67
* hot chocolate or hot cider
* cups
* spoons
* extra blankets and pillows

Optional:

* set and costumes to go with the script

Do Ahead ≫ Gather a few people to form a readers' theater group and practice the "Tell Me a Story" script. If you have kids who are strong readers, include at least one of them or let them read all the roles. Ask your volunteers to be ready with some favorite children's books. In your publicity to the congregation, ask everyone to bring blankets and pillows and perhaps some favorite books. Younger kids may even want to come in pajamas.

Option! ≫ Have everyone pass around their favorite books for others to look at.

Get It Done ≫ 1. **Set up the staging area.** Create a simple readers' theater set with stools for readers to sit on and music stands to hold scripts. Make sure you're in an area with good light for the readers even when you dim the lights in the rest of the room. If you'd like, you can make a more elaborate set to go along with the Tell Me a Story script. Actors can wear costumes and carry props while they sit on stools or move around on the set.

2. **Welcome participants.** As families and individuals arrive, welcome them and ask them to get comfortable with blankets and pillows on the floor. If you have a fireplace in the room you're using, build a cozy fire. Ask some volunteers to serve hot chocolate or hot cider—or both!

3. **Share favorite books.** Invite everyone to show the books they brought. See if anyone would like to read a children's book or part of a chapter book. Depending on the ability of your participants, you may want to have your readers' theater group do all the reading so everyone can hear and the reading goes smoothly. However, you may prefer to let kids experience the pride of reading for themselves, offering gentle help as needed. Make a point to ask adults to share about their favorite stories whether or not they brought books.

4. **Present Tell Me a Story.** See if anyone needs refills on hot chocolate or cider, then turn down the lights and let everyone settle in for the main presentation. Introduce the drama by saying: **We've shared lots of favorite stories. Now it's time to hear about God's story. We're going to need your help. Whenever you hear someone say, "That's not the end of the story," that means it's your turn to say, "I love a good story!" Practice the cue and response, and then begin the readers' theater presentation.**

5. **Thank your performers.** Give a round of applause for the readers. Let people get refills on hot drinks. Then enjoy the Take It Home time together.

> ## Family Connections
> - Kids find out what stories parents like.
> - Kids and parents do something they can do again at home— read together.
> - The whole faith family hears God's story together.

Take It Home

> **Bible Verse:** "Your word, O LORD, is eternal; it stands firm in the heavens" (Psalm 119:89).

We've heard a lot of stories together today. We just heard the best story of all—God's story. Ask: **Tell me about your favorite part of God's story.** In the process of affirming answers, highlight the main points of the story of redemption: Adam and Eve sinned, but God still loved them. God chose His people and loved them no matter what they did. He sent Jesus into the world to die for our sins so we could live with Him forever. We have the Holy Spirit to help us please God, and someday Jesus will come again. **It's all exciting stuff!**

God has used all kinds of people to tell His story. In Bible times, prophets told people what God wanted them to do. Sometimes God sent angels with special messages. And finally He sent Jesus so the world would understand how much He loves us. And now we have the Bible so we can read the story over and over and tell it to each other.

Ask a volunteer to read Psalm 119:89 from a Bible. Ask: **What does it mean that God's Word is eternal and stands firm in the heavens?** God is forever. What He says is always true. It will never change.

We are God's people. We keep on telling His story. People still need to know the good news of God's kingdom and how to be part of it. We have a great story to tell and it never gets old!

Close with a prayer thanking God for the great story of His wonderful love.

Tell Me A Story

Readers: Narrator, Angel, Shepherd, Prophet, and Disciple

Narrator: We have a great story for you! But you're part of it. Remember, when you hear me say, "That's not the end of the story," you answer, "I love a good story."

Angel: In the beginning, God created the heavens and the earth. He made Adam and Eve and gave them a beautiful place to live. They had a perfect relationship with God.

Prophet: But Adam and Eve made a big mistake. They did the one thing God told them not to do. Now their relationship with God was broken.

Narrator: That's not the end of the story. *Pause for response: I love a good story.*

Prophet: God still loved Adam and Eve. Soon the world was full of people. God chose one man to be His special friend. The man's name was Abraham.

Angel: God made a promise to Abraham. He promised that Abraham would have a big, big family. And through one of the people in Abraham's family, the relationship people have with God would be fixed.

Prophet: God loved Abraham. He gave him a son named Isaac.

Shepherd: And Isaac had two sons, Esau and Jacob.

Angel: And Jacob had 12 sons.

Prophet: Pretty soon Abraham's family had hundreds of people.

Angel: And then thousands.

Shepherd: And then millions.

Narrator: God chose Abraham's family to be His special people. He loved them! But that's not the end of the story. *Pause for response: I love a good story.*

Angel: God led His people into a new land.

Prophet: He gave them everything thing they needed.

Shepherd: God was like a shepherd taking care of His sheep.

Prophet: God sent messengers so the people would know what God wanted them to do.

Angel: God guided His people. He showed them His way.

Shepherd: But God's people got stubborn. They wanted to do things their own way. They sinned against God.

Prophet: They worshiped false gods.

Angel: They turned away from the true God.

Shepherd: The sheep didn't listen to the shepherd.

Prophet: But still God loved His people.

Angel: Still God wanted to be close to His people.

Shepherd: Still God wanted to fix the relationship with His people.

Narrator: Hundreds of years went by. But that's not the end of the story. *Pause for response: I love a good story.*

Prophet: God used prophets to tell the people He would fix what went wrong.

Shepherd: He wanted His people to be close to Him again.

Angel: He wanted His people to live with Him forever!

Narrator: The people still wandered away from God. But that's not the end of the story. *Pause for response: I love a good story.*

Angel: God had a plan.

Shepherd: A good plan.

Prophet: A plan to save His people from their sin.

Shepherd: God decided to send a Savior.

Angel: The angel Gabriel visited Mary with an exciting message. She would be the mother of the Savior!

Shepherd: When the Savior was born, shepherds in the field were the first ones to find out the good news.

Angel: Angels in the sky praised God.

Shepherd: The shepherds ran to Bethlehem to see the baby Jesus.

Narrator: Jesus came to save us from our sins. But that's not the end of the story. *Pause for response: I love a good story.*

Shepherd: Jesus was the good shepherd. He loved the people and healed the sick.

Prophet: Jesus was a great teacher, too. He taught the people about the kingdom of God.

Angel: This was how the people could be close to God again.

Prophet: Jesus' message was to repent, to stop sinning, to turn around and go God's way.

Shepherd: Jesus had 12 special friends, the disciples.

Disciple: The disciples helped spread the good news about the kingdom of God. Many people believed the good news.

Shepherd: Many people wanted to be sheep in God's flock.

Disciple: But not everyone was happy about the stories Jesus told.

Prophet: Some people wanted Jesus dead!

Disciple: They accused Jesus of things He didn't do. The punishment was death!

Angel: But this was all part of God's plan.

Disciple: It was all part of the way God was fixing the broken relationship people had with Him.

Shepherd: The good shepherd died for the sheep. Jesus died on a cross for us.

Narrator: Jesus died to save us from our sins. This was all part of God's plan. But this was not the end of the story. *Pause for response: I love a good story.*

Disciple: The disciples were heartbroken when Jesus died.

Angel: But three days later, angels met Jesus' friends at the tomb.

Disciple: The empty tomb!

Angel: God raised Jesus from the dead!

Disciple: Now the disciples had some more amazing news to tell.

Shepherd: Jesus' friends kept spreading the good news.

Narrator: Jesus went back to Heaven to be with His Father. But that's not the end of the story. *Pause for response: I love a good story.*

Disciple: Before He went to Heaven, Jesus told His friends to keep spreading the good news.

Angel: God sent the Holy Spirit to help them.

Disciple: The disciples told their friends, and they told their friends, and they told their friends.

Angel: Soon thousands of people believed.

Disciple: All the people who believed became the church.

Shepherd: God was still taking care of His people. God loves us!

Disciple: Now all of us are part of God's story. We're the church. When we believe in Jesus, we are part of God's family.

Prophet: Some day Jesus is going to come again.

Angel: Then everyone will know the truth about Jesus.

Prophet: The world will end. Only Heaven will last forever.

Narrator: And that will be the end of the story!

Copyright © 2007 by Susan Martins Miller. Permission is granted to reproduce this page for ministry purposes only—not for resale.

Draw Me a Picture, Please

God made a wonderfully creative world—and He made us in His image. We enjoy creative expression as we reflect His glory. This is one way to worship and celebrate God's goodness. Use this gathering to encourage families and groups to give back to God the creativity He has given them.

Set It Up

Supplies:

* butcher paper
* masking tape
* markers
* Bibles
* copies of Story Starters on page 70

Optional:

* copies of Use This on page 71
* assortment of drama props and costumes

Do Ahead ≫ Choose the Bible stories you want families or groups to illustrate. If you wish, choose Bible stories according to a theme you want to emphasize, such as all stories of Jesus or all stories about Moses or seasonal stories. Make enough copies of pages 70 for each group to have one. Page 71 is optional. Make copies if you choose to use it.

Option! ≫ Collect props for optional dramatic presentations of Bible stories.

Get It Done ≫ 1. **Prepare the space.** Cut strips of butcher paper about four feet long. Use the masking tape to affix the paper to walls securely. Put a bucket of markers at each station. Plan on families or small groups of up to six to eight people working at each station.

2. **Welcome participants.** As families and individuals arrive, have everyone gather in a central spot for instructions.

3. **Explain the project.** Each family or group will illustrate a Bible story. Each group will receive a list of elements that must be included in the illustration. Each group can illustrate the story in the style of its choice—one large drawing, comic-strip style, using symbolism, or any other idea.

Distribute copies of Story Starters on page 70 to help jumpstart group members' thinking. For a fun and challenging twist, distribute Use This from page 71 that includes a list of items that must be used in the illustration. Another idea is to let groups illustrate backdrops to their stories and prepare a brief drama to present to the large group.

4. **Read the stories.** Have families or groups gather at stations and read their stories together from the Bible.

5. **Illustrate the stories.** Allow time for groups to work. If you'd like, play some lively music in the background.

6. **Visit stations.** When everyone has finished, invite groups to go around the room and see the other illustrations that were drawn. If any groups have prepared a drama, let them present it for everyone. If your group is large, they can present several times as groups come through the station.

7. **Gather your group together.** Enjoy the Take It Home time together. If groups worked in families, let the families take home their masterpieces. Or you might want to find a place to display the artwork for a couple of weeks so the entire congregation can see it.

Family Connections

- Families explore Bible stories together.
- Kids and parents celebrate the creativity God has given them.
- Families build bridges with each other as they work together in groups.

Take It Home

> **Bible Verse:** "These commandments that I give you today are to be upon your hearts. Impress them on your children. Talk about them when you sit at home and when you walk along the road, when you lie down and when you get up" (Deuteronomy 6:6, 7).

As the group gathers, ask these questions about the experience:
What was the most fun part of illustrating a Bible story?
What was the hardest part?
What did you learn about each other while doing this activity together?
What did you learn about God while doing this together?
Say: **God is an amazing God. We see His creativity all around us in the things He made in the world. It's fun sometimes to reflect God's creativity with a little of our own.**

We illustrated Bible stories. This is one way to pass on the good news about God in our families. Let's read some Bible verses about that. Ask a volunteer to read Deuteronomy 6:6, 7 from a Bible. **These verses remind us how important it is for families to learn God's way together.**

Ask: **Tell me about a time when your family can learn God's way together at home.** Listen to answers. Ask: **Parents, how can we impress God's way on the hearts of our kids?** Listen to answers. Ask: **Kids, when is a good time to ask your parents a question about God's way?**

Close with a prayer that asks God to bless the families and individuals in your church as they share God's way with each other.

Story Starters

What's your favorite part of this story?
What's the most exciting part of this story?
What would you like people to learn from this story?
What are the main actions in this story?
What would you do if you were in this story?

Story Starters

What's your favorite part of this story?
What's the most exciting part of this story?
What would you like people to learn from this story?
What are the main actions in this story?
What would you do if you were in this story?

Story Starters

What's your favorite part of this story?
What's the most exciting part of this story?
What would you like people to learn from this story?
What are the main actions in this story?
What would you do if you were in this story?

Story Starters

What's your favorite part of this story?
What's the most exciting part of this story?
What would you like people to learn from this story?
What are the main actions in this story?
What would you do if you were in this story?

Copyright © 2007 by Susan Martins Miller. Permission is granted to reproduce this page for ministry purposes only—not for resale.

USe THiS

- an animal
- a household item
- a plant
- signs with words
- a clock

- a road
- something that shines
- squares
- triangles

USe THiS

- an animal
- a household item
- a plant
- signs with words
- a clock

- a road
- something that shines
- squares
- triangles

USe THiS

- an animal
- a household item
- a plant
- signs with words
- a clock

- a road
- something that shines
- squares
- triangles

USe THiS

- an animal
- a household item
- a plant
- signs with words
- a clock

- a road
- something that shines
- squares
- triangles

Copyright © 2007 by Susan Martins Miller. Permission is granted to reproduce this page for ministry purposes only—not for resale.

Gotta Love That Baby

Children are a precious gift from God. Sometimes, though, the circumstances of birth are not what God intended, and parents need extra help surrounding a new baby with love and hope. Ask families to bring gifts and throw a baby shower for an organization that ministers to unmarried or low-income mothers to let the moms know their babies are precious.

Set It Up

Supplies:

- copies of Baby Stuff on page 74 printed on colorful paper
- gift wrap
- clear tape
- scissors
- pictures of babies
- construction paper

Optional:

- lullaby music

Do Ahead

Talk with a representative of an organization that ministers to young, unmarried mothers or low-income mothers and find out what the ministry needs or what kinds of gifts they recommend for the moms and babies. Publicize this list along with information about when the baby shower will be held. Emphasize that this baby shower is for the whole family. Ask families to bring pictures of family members as babies.

Option!

Invite families with baby shower invitations and serve baby shower refreshments.

Get It Done

1. **Choose your theme.** As you talk with a ministry representative, you might learn that some gifts can benefit moms and babies over and over again. If the ministry is residential, such as a place where new moms can get on their feet for a few months, gifts such as bedding, dishes, books or toys will stay with the ministry as the moms come and go. Other items can go with the moms when they leave, such as a few quality toys or books or baby clothes. Decide if you'd like to focus on one kind of gift or the other; you can do both if you'd like. Whatever your decision, make sure to communicate to members of the congregation the kind of gift needed.

2. **Decorate and set up.** Use pictures of babies to decorate the area where you will hold your baby shower. These can be pictures of your own friends and family as babies or you can cut them out of magazines. Glue or tape them onto colorful construction paper backgrounds and put them up around the room. Set up several wrapping stations with gift wrap, tape, scissors and copies of p. 74.

3. **Welcome participants.** As families and individuals arrive, direct them to a gathering area. If you'd like, play lullaby music in the background.

4. **Feature the ministry that will receive your gifts.** Explain the ministry of the organization you have selected. If possible, invite a representative of the organization to join you in person. Help family members, especially kids, understand how their gifts will be used, whether the gifts are items for the organization, such as bedding and dishes, or items for the moms and babies.

5. **Get wrapping!** At a baby shower, you open gifts and pass them around. This time, pass them around first, and then wrap them up. Let everyone wrap the gifts they brought and attach one of the tags from page 74. Point out that the tags have space for personal messages. Wrappers can simply sign their names or write as much as they like.

6. **Enjoy refreshments.** If you're serving baby shower refreshments, enjoy them now. Look for ways to get kids involved in serving, such as cutting cake or distributing drinks.

7. **Gather your group.** Enjoy the Take It Home time together.

> ## Family Connections
>
> - Parents will naturally talk about when their kids were babies.
> - Kids will understand that not everyone has the things they take for granted.
> - Parents model generosity by giving gifts and getting nothing back.

Take It Home

> **Bible Verse:** "For you created my inmost being; you knit me together in my mother's womb" (Psalm 139:13).

Find out who brought baby pictures. If not every family has some, use the magazine pictures you used for decorations.

Ask: **When you look at these pictures, whom do you think the babies look like?** Allow some time for families to look at their pictures and talk about this question. Even if you're using magazine pictures or have adopted children in your group, they can still talk about someone the baby's features remind them of.

God sure gets creative when He creates babies, doesn't He? Every baby is different. Even identical twins who look alike have some differences. God loves every single baby He makes.

Ask a volunteer to read Psalm 139:13 from a Bible. Ask: **What do you think "inmost being" means?** Some kids will think on a literal level. Others will talk about the thoughts and emotions they have on the inside that make them individuals.

God puts every one of us in a special place inside our mothers' bodies. No matter where a baby is born or what the family has, God loves that baby even before it is born. Our gifts are going to help some mothers remember that God loves their babies.

Close with a prayer time for the ministry that will receive your gifts. Invite both kids and adults to offer sentence prayers and then close.

you are
precious to God!

THIS gift is a gift of
God's love to you.

"I praise you because I am fearfully
and wonderfully made."
—Psalm 139:14

Copyright © 2007 by Susan Martins Miller. Permission is granted to reproduce this page for ministry purposes only—not for resale.

Holy Week with the Family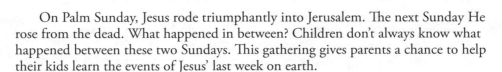

On Palm Sunday, Jesus rode triumphantly into Jerusalem. The next Sunday He rose from the dead. What happened in between? Children don't always know what happened between these two Sundays. This gathering gives parents a chance to help their kids learn the events of Jesus' last week on earth.

Set It Up

Supplies:

- copies of Holy Week Family Book on pages 77 and 78
- card stock
- hole punch
- large colorful paper clips
- markers
- Bibles
- construction paper
- paper towel tube
- marble

Optional:

- assorted decorating supplies, such as stickers, glitter, sequins, gel pens

Do Ahead ▷ Step 1 (below) lists 15 events in the last week of Jesus' life. Your group will try to put these in the correct order. Choose as many of them as you would like to use and write the words in large letters on construction paper. Depending on the time available at your gathering, you may want to read the Scripture passages that go with the signs you make.

Option! ▷ Put the descriptions and references on separate papers and have families read the passages to match up the descriptions.

Get It Done ▷ 1. **Make event signs.** On construction paper, write in large letters the following descriptions of Jesus' last week—one per paper. Mix up the signs.

Jesus comes to Jerusalem (Matt. 21:1-11), Jesus clears the temple (Matt. 21:18, 19), Mary anoints Jesus' feet (Matt. 26:6-13), Judas plans to betray Jesus (Matt 26:14, 15), Judas washes his disciples' feet (John 13:1-20), Jesus gives a new command to love (John 13:34, 35), Jesus predicts Peter's denial (John 13:31-38), Judas betrays Jesus (John 18:2-12), Jesus goes to trial with Jewish leaders (John 18:13-24), Peter denies Jesus (18:15-18, 25-27), Jesus goes to trial before Pilate (John 18:28-38), soldiers mock Jesus (Matt. 27:27-30), Jesus is crucified (John 19:16-30), Jesus is buried (John 19:39-42), Jesus is risen (John 20:1-10).

2. **Put the signs in order.** When your group has gathered, explain that they'll be learning about what happened to Jesus during His last week on earth. Show the signs that you've made and say that the group will be putting them in order from left to right. The kids will draw from the pile of signs one at a time. It's up to the parents to decide where each sign should go in relation to the others. Kids can stay up front and hold signs or you can tape them to a wall. Use the list in Step 1 as your key to the correct order.

Family Connections

- Parents create a tool to talk with kids about Jesus.

- Families read the Bible and pray together.

- The faith family remembers Jesus together.

3. **Make family devotional books.** Give each family or group a set of handouts. Cut out the long strips and fold them in half. Next lay the pages facing up with the Monday page on the bottom, then Tuesday, then Wednesday, and then Thursday on top. Fold the stack in half. Punch two holes a few inches apart near the folded edge. Insert large paper clips through the holes to hold the booklet together. Decorate the outside covers. Each day during Holy Week the family can read the passage for that day and talk about the questions. Then they can write a family prayer on the blank page for that day.

4. **Gather your group.** Enjoy the Take It Home time together.

Take It Home

Bible Verse: "For the Son of Man came to seek and to save what was lost" (Luke 19:10).

Have you heard the saying, "There's light at the end of the tunnel"? Hold an empty paper towel tube up to your eye. **If I look through this tube, I see light at the other end. Inside the tunnel may seem dark, but on the other end it's light again.**

Set the tube on a table and take out a marble. Have a few kids come up and try to "flick" the marble through the tunnel from one end to the other.

Say: **Jesus' last week on earth was something like a tunnel. It started out on Palm Sunday. Jesus came into Jerusalem and the people praised Him. But as the week went on, things got darker. Jesus knew that pretty soon He would die. He spent time with His disciples one last time. Then He was arrested and crucified. His friends laid His body in a tomb. That was the darkest part of the tunnel.**

Ask a volunteer to read Luke 19:10. Ask: **What does this verse tell us about the tunnel Jesus went through?** Jesus' death had a purpose. God sent Him into the world to save the lost—us.

Roll the marble through the paper towel tube again. **There was light at the end of the tunnel! Jesus died on Friday and on Sunday He rose from the dead. When His friends went to the tomb, it was empty!**

Holy Week gives us a time to remember the tunnel Jesus went through, and to thank God for the light of the resurrection.

Tuesday

Read Matthew 26:6, 7
- How did pouring expensive perfume on Jesus show how the woman felt?
- How do we show Jesus how we feel about Him?

In the space below, write a prayer telling Jesus how you feel about Him.

Saturday

Read John 19:40-42
- What did Jesus' friends do with His body?
- What do we wait for on the night before Easter?

In the space below, write a prayer thanking God for sacrificing His Son for you.

Monday

Read Matthew 21:12, 13
- Why did Jesus clear out the temple?
- How does God want us to worship Him?

In the space below, write a prayer asking God to keep your hearts clean.

Sunday

Read Matthew 28:1-7
- What did the women find at the tomb?
- How can the angel's words help us?

In the space below, write a prayer thanking God for the power He showed when He raised Jesus from the dead.

Thursday

Read John 13:34, 35
- What command did Jesus give His disciples?
- How do we show love to one another?

In the space below, write a prayer asking God to help you show His love to other people.

Copyright © 2007 by Susan Martins Miller. Permission is granted to reproduce this page for ministry purposes only—not for resale.

Wednesday

Read John 15:9, 10
- What does Jesus want us to do?
- How do we show that we love Jesus?

In the space below, write a prayer asking God to keep you close to Him.

Friday

Read Luke 23:44-47
- What did the centurion realize when Jesus died?
- Why are you thankful that the Son of God died?

In the space below, write a prayer confessing sins and asking God's forgiveness.

Plant New Life ◎

Spring brings buds and leaves and blooming colors. The weather warms up. We spend more time outside. Gardeners dig in the earth anticipating the rewards that will come a few weeks later. Gardens, whether plants or vegetables, are a wonderful way to celebrate God's provision and share it with others. Use this community garden as a service project for your congregation.

Set It Up

Supplies:

* sign-up sheet (See page 81 for header.)
* clipboard and pen
* seeds or starter plants
* gardening tools
* soil enrichments
* water or refreshments
* Bible
* copies of Garden Tenders on page 81

Optional:

* supplies for scarecrow

Do Ahead ❯ Use the header from page 81 to create a sign-up sheet. List all the weeks from plant date to harvest time and have families sign up to tend the garden for a week at a time. Prepare copies of Garden Tenders on page 81 with information specific to your situation.

Option! ❯ Ask families to contribute starter plants to the garden.

Get It Done ❯ 1. **Decide what to plant.** You might want to have an organizational meeting ahead of time and involve others in deciding what kind of garden to plant. Flowers can beautify a community area, such as the median of a major street. Vegetables can yield a harvest for a community food pantry and give needy families fresh food. Choose plants that will grow well in your geographic area. Consult a local nursery if you're unsure.

2. **Explain the project.** Meet at the planting site. Explain to your group what and where you will be planting. Having a sketch show rows and plants is a good idea. This does not have to be elaborate, just clear enough so everyone shares the same mental picture.

3. **Dig and plant.** Time to get to work! Distribute tools and get going. Make sure everyone has a task, whether it's marking off the rows, digging, enriching the soil, planting, watering, or serving refreshments. Pair parents or adults with young children to work together. Younger kids love to help, so make sure they have a meaningful contribution rather than merely watching adults work. Make this a time for kids to learn some gardening skills rather than being in a hurry to get the work done. Use as many "dig and plant" sessions as you need for the entire garden.

4. **Sign up.** Put the sign-up sheet on a clipboard and circulate it. Make sure everyone understands the expectations. Do you want them to water the garden? Pull weeds? How many times a week? Make sure that each week is covered. You may also want to offer this opportunity to other individuals or families who were not able to participate in the planting session. Distribute copies of Garden Tenders (p. 81) so everyone has a reminder of the opportunity for ministry.

Family Connections

- Kids and parents serve together.

- Kids see parents giving up their time for others.

- Kids and adults bond through a time of mentoring.

5. **Enjoy refreshments.** Gardening is hard work. Remind everyone to stay hydrated along the way, especially if the day is warm.

6. **Gather your group.** Enjoy the Take It Home time together.

Take It Home

Bible Verse: "What shall we say the kingdom of God is like, or what parable shall we use to describe it? It is like a mustard seed, which is the smallest seed you plant in the ground. Yet when planted, it grows and becomes the largest of all garden plants, with such big branches that the birds of the air can perch in its shade" (Mark 4:30-32).

How many different plants do you think the Bible mentions? More than we can name! But here are a few. Name as many of these plants as you'd like, or see if people in your group can name any of them. Acacia balm calamus, barley, cedar, cinnamon, beans, briars, broom tree, coriander, date, fir, flax, garlic, gourds, grain, grapes, herbs, hyssop, leeks, lilies, lentils, mandrakes, mulberry tree, mustard tree, oak, onion, palm, pine tree, pomegranate, reeds, rose of Sharon, vine, willow, apple tree, figs.

Jesus talked about one kind of plant in particular. Ask a volunteer to read Mark 4:30-32 from a Bible. Ask: **What does this passage tell us about the kingdom of God?** It grows from a small seed and becomes huge.

These seeds (or starter plants) **that we put in the ground today are starting out small. But we planted them to be a blessing to people in our community. So we're going to water them and tend them to make the blessing as big as we can. This is one way we can show God's love and kingdom to the people in our community who need to know Him.**

Close with a group prayer time for God to bless lives through the results of your community garden.

Garden of Blessing

Sign up to take care of our community garden for one week.

Make copies of these garden instructions for everyone who participates. Use the space to give specific instructions about what to do, where to find tools, and so on.

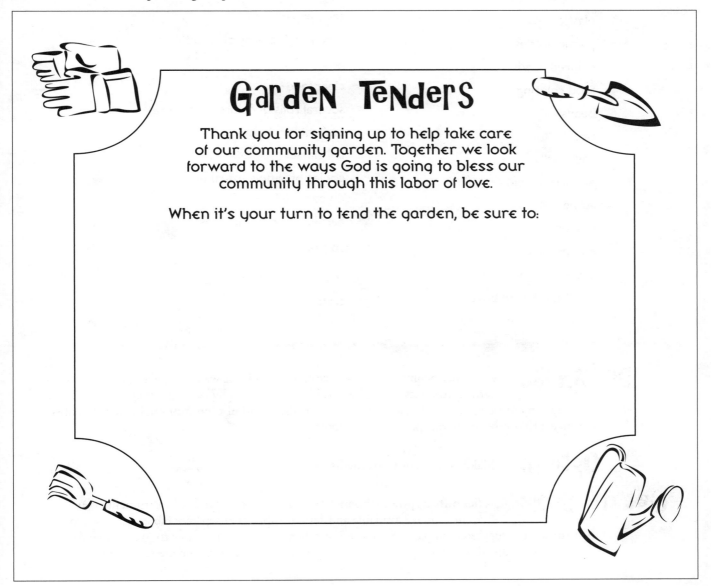

Garden Tenders

Thank you for signing up to help take care of our community garden. Together we look forward to the ways God is going to bless our community through this labor of love.

When it's your turn to tend the garden, be sure to:

Copyright © 2007 by Susan Martins Miller. Permission is granted to reproduce this page for ministry purposes only—not for resale.

Make a Joyful Noise

The psalms tell us to make a joyful noise! This should be right up your kids' alley. Making instruments gives everyone a chance to celebrate God's gift of creativity at the same time. These joyful noise instruments can be made simply by kids or more elaborately by adults.

Set It Up

Supplies:

- plastic cups
- plastic bottles
- colored beads
- food coloring
- beans
- rice
- jingle bells
- elasticized gold thread
- string
- scissors
- dowel rods
- drinking straws
- small cardboard boxes
- construction paper
- felt
- sand paper
- 1″ x 4″ x 4″ pieces of wood
- glue
- clear tape
- several rolls of colored tape
- embroidery hoops
- tall glasses
- copies of Simple Instruments on pages 84 and 85
- hardware odds and ends

Optional:

- stickers
- craft paint

Do Ahead ≫ Ask other people to help you collect clear plastic water or soda bottles, small cardboard boxes, and glass bottles so you have plenty to go around. If you'd like, you can cut items such as felt and sand paper to size ahead of time. You might want to enlist volunteers to oversee work on specific instruments.

Option! ≫ Make samples of instruments.

Get It Done ≫ 1. **Set out supplies.** Choose how many different kinds of instruments you want to make available and set out supplies at separate tables. Choose from the instruments suggested on pages 84 and 85 or others that you know how to make. If you'd like, put photocopied instructions at each station. If possible, set up a separate station for each kind of instrument. Try not to have more than two projects going on at the same table, just to keep supplies organized. Put items such as beans, rice, and beads in small bowls.

2. **Welcome participants.** Ask a couple of older kids to be greeters. As participants arrive, direct them to the various tables to look around and choose what to work on. Samples made ahead of time will help people choose quickly.

3. **Make instruments.** Decide how much time to allow for working on instruments. Encourage adults to make more sophisticated versions. Anyone who thinks of a way to improve on the idea using the supplies at hand is free to do so. Emphasize that each instrument will be different from all the rest. If time allows and you have enough supplies, participants can make more than one instrument. Give a couple of warnings when time is nearly up so participants have a chance to finish up what they're doing.

> **Family Connections**
> - Parents relax and let out their playful sides!
> - Families worship together.
> - Families have visible reminders of their time together.

4. **Clean up.** You'll have lots to put away. Ask kids to help you sort leftover supplies and clean up trash.

5. **Gather your group.** Enjoy the Take It Home time together with your instruments.

Take It Home

> **Bible Verse:** "Come, let us sing for joy to the Lord; let us shout aloud to the Rock of our salvation" (Psalm 95:1).

Ahead of time, select some praise and worship songs to sing together. Be sure to include some that younger kids will know as well as more complex ones for adults. Choose songs with a strong rhythm. Be open to other suggestions as you worship together.

Invite volunteers to show their instruments and give demonstrations. Ask kids to tell you why they selected the instruments they did and what their favorite part of the process was.

Then put the instruments to use with a time of praise and worship music. Sing for as much time as you have available.

Ask a volunteer to read Psalm 95:1 from a Bible. **We've certainly been doing exactly what this verse tells us to do—make a joyful noise. But not every noise we make is joyful.** Ask: **What are some noises we make that aren't so joyful?** Participants may mention things like grumbling or arguing or activities that make unpleasant noises like construction work. Any answer is fine.

We have a lot of noises in our lives. Sometimes we can hardly hear ourselves think! But God wants us to come away from all that noise and make a good noise, a joyful noise, that's just for Him. He doesn't require fancy instruments. What He wants is happy hearts that are grateful for what He gives us. And we can do that!

Close by playing the instruments along with one more praise song.

Sand Blocks

Materials needed: wood pieces, felt, sandpaper, glue, heavy books or other heavy objects

Sand away any rough edges on the wood. Cut felt to fit wood blocks and glue on. Then add a piece of sandpaper on top of the felt. Place books or other heavy objects on the blocks while they dry.

Jingle Bracelets

Materials needed: elastic ponytail holders, elasticized gold thread, jingle bells

Using the elasticized thread, tie four jingle bells onto each bracelet, spaced equally around the ponytail holder.

Bean Shakers

Materials needed: plastic soda bottles; dried beans, peas, lentils, or rice

Make sure the bottles are clean and dry. Fill the bottles about half full of beans or rice. Shakers will make different sounds depending on what you put in them. Screw on the bottle lids tightly. If you want, you can use superglue to make sure lids won't come off.

Jingle Bars

Materials needed: 6″ dowel rods, 6″ lengths of string, tape, jingle bells

Tie a piece of string onto the end of a dowel. Tape in place if necessary. Tie jingle bells at the end of the string. You can use several strings with one dowel if you like.

Copyright © 2007 by Susan Martins Miller. Permission is granted to reproduce this page for ministry purposes only—not for resale.

Hardware Hoops

Materials needed: small embroidery hoops; odds and ends of hardware such as paper clips, washers, old keys; string; tape

You can use anything metal that makes a fun sound. Use string and tape to hang hardware from the hoop so everything jangles. If you'd like, wrap duct tape around the hoop to make everything gray or silver.

Shaker Cups

Materials needed: clear plastic cups, colored beads, colorful tape

Put some colored beads in one clear plastic cup. Set another cup upside down on top of the first one and use colorful tape to hold the cups together so you can shake them.

Pitch Bottles

Materials needed: glass bottles, water, food coloring

Put a different amount of water in each bottle so that when you blow over them they each make a different musical pitch. Adjust the water levels to get the pitches you want. Add a drop of food coloring to each bottle for color. See if you can play a simple tune with the pitches you have created.

Straw Scrapers

Materials needed: drinking straws, small cardboard boxes, construction paper, glue

Cover a small box with construction paper. Glue a row of straws to the cardboard box. Make a musical sound by dragging a single straw across the surface of the row of straws.

Copyright © 2007 by Susan Martins Miller. Permission is granted to reproduce this page for ministry purposes only—not for resale.

Not Your Father's Church Picnic

The traditional annual church picnic was a time for a leisurely meal, fun and games, and an opportunity to socialize and perhaps even meet someone new. Your congregation may enjoy something with more pizzazz, but the benefits to congregational life endure. Plan a church picnic, whether traditional or with a modern spin, and give families time to get to know each other and build bridges of support.

Set It Up

Supplies:

* food (See Step 2 below.)
* plates, forks, cups
* theme decorations (See Step 3 below.)
* game supplies (See Step 4 below.)

Do Ahead ⟫ If you're going to hold the picnic somewhere other than your church grounds, be sure to call well in advance to reserve space in a park or other covered eating area. If you plan to go to a theme park, check for off-season rates for late spring or early fall.

Option! ⟫ Crank homemade ice cream to enjoy after fun and games.

Get It Done ⟫ 1. **Delegate the work.** You don't have to do it all yourself. Plan on a food committee, a games committee, a set-up team, and a clean-up team. If possible, meet with everyone ahead of time to share your vision of how a church picnic can inspire relationships within your congregation.

2. **Plan the food.** The first thing that comes to mind is probably the predictable potluck where every family brings a dish to share, or the church provides meat to grill and everyone brings side dishes. If this is the best idea for your group, consider putting a spin on it with a food theme—Mexican, Italian, Asian, or any food heritage of your choice. In your publicity, provide some ideas for dishes that fall into the category you select. But you do have other options for food. See page 88 for more ideas.

3. **Plan the theme.** Even if you don't use a food theme, you may want to have a theme for the general atmosphere of the picnic, such as retro, Hawaiian, Caribbean, futuristic, safari, or beach (even without water). Let your imagination run wild to come up with a theme that makes people curious to come.

4. **Plan the games.** The traditional church picnic involves group games that many people can participate in. Softball, volleyball, tug-o-war, and relay games are always good starts. But you could also put together some outdoor carnival games or a string of TV game show knock-offs that let some participate and many others enjoy. Play a version of the old "Newlywed Game" with couples married for varying lengths of time, or pair up a parent and child to see how well they know each other. You could also rent inflatable games for kids to enjoy. Include some quiet table games like checkers and chess and candy bar Bingo for the less-athletic members. Encourage intergenerational play as much as possible without being too concerned about competition. See page 88 for more ideas.

5. **Gather your group.** Designate a time for everyone to gather for a brief devotional time. Make sure to do this early enough that you're not interrupting games and that people have not begun to leave. Enjoy the Take It Home time together.

> ### Family Connections
>
> - Parents and kids spend time together.
> - Kids interact with the larger faith family.
> - The whole faith family shares fun memories.

Take It Home

Bible Verse: "My purpose is that they may be encouraged in heart and united in love, so that they may have the full riches of complete understanding, in order that they may know the mystery of God, namely, Christ" (Colossians 2:2).

Ask the picnickers about their favorite foods, favorite desserts, or favorite games—anything about the picnic day they'd like to talk about.

Ask: **Is it more fun to go on a picnic by yourself or with other people?** Responses will vary, but most will prefer a picnic with others.

Ask: **What good feelings do you get when you go on a picnic with friends?**

When we're together with other people we care about, we encourage each other and show our love for each other. This might be in your family, with friends, or with a whole bunch of people like today. Let's read a Bible verse about what God's people can do for each other.

Have a volunteer read Colossians 2:2 from a Bible. Ask: **What does this verse say we can do for each other?** We can encourage each other; be united in love. Ask: **According to this verse, why does God want us to encourage each other and be united in love?** So we can know Christ better, more fully.

Name someone you talked to today or played with today who helped you know Christ better. Pause for answers.

We don't have to have a special meeting to encourage each other or be united in love. God wants us to have these kinds of relationships no matter what we're doing. We can eat together, play together, talk together, laugh together, and all the while we show the love of Jesus among us and encourage each other to follow him more closely.

Roast a pig!

Arrange with a butcher for the pig. Google "pig roast" on the Internet to find ways to cook the pig. This likely will require an overnight crew to tend to the pig as it cooks. If someone has an RV, arrange to bring it to the cooking site and have your crew hang out there. Recruit a crew of fathers and kids, teenagers, all men, or some other group. Make a special relational time out of the experience.

Boxed Lunch

Generations ago, young women prepared boxed lunches and young men bid on the boxes without knowing who had prepared them. Try doing this with salads or deserts. Have members box up the food in decorated packages or leave them visible. Let purchasers guess who made the dishes. Then the person who prepared the basket and the person who purchased it can enjoy it together. This is a great way to raise money for a special cause.

Sports Event

Organize a group outing to a local athletic event. This doesn't have to be a professional team. Perhaps your area has a minor league baseball team, for instance. Have a tailgate party in the parking lot before the game.

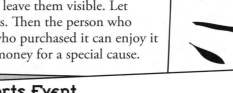

Carnival Games

The Internet is loaded with ideas for outdoor carnival games: balloon darts, cake walk, hula toss, tic-tac-toe toss, clothespin toss, beanbag toss through the clown's mouth, dunk tanks, etc. Many of these games can be made easily out of thin plywood and paint. Keep things as simple or as elaborate as you want. Make them once and use them over and over. Don't forget the prizes!

Cater the Food

Busy families appreciate a meal in which they don't have to contribute. Work with a local restaurant or caterer for a simple but satisfying meal that is work-free for the members of your church.

Missions Picnic

Combine a missions or service emphasis with the church picnic. Set up several tables or stations that people can visit throughout the day to learn more about missionaries your church supports around the world or of local service opportunities.

Copyright © 2007 by Susan Martins Miller. Permission is granted to reproduce this page for ministry purposes only—not for resale.

Will You Play With Me? Family Nights

Many parents want to spend more "quality time" with their kids, but they're not sure what that is, or it's hard to corral everyone to do something together as a family. This gathering gives families a chance to plan their family nights and get excited about spending time together in simple yet memorable ways.

Set It Up

Supplies:

* copies of Family Night Planner on page 91
* pencils
* index cards
* CD player and music

Do Ahead ≫ Write the following family night ideas on individual index cards: reading, cooking, watching movies, playing board games, bowling, hosting a dinner, making crafts, playing video games, making homemade cards, planting and tending a garden, making gifts to give away, building a fort, making a family tree, singing or making music, memorizing Bible verses, looking at family photos, looking at baby books, making a family prayer journal, putting together a jigsaw puzzle, and cleaning up old toys to give away.

Option! ≫ Make larger signs with words from the list above and use as decorations around the room.

Get It Done ≫ 1. **Make activity cards.** As participants enter, have each person write on an index card something he would like to do as a family or with a group of friends. This can be anything from playing with blocks to traveling to Hawaii. Have adult helpers or older kids on hand to help young children with their ideas. Make sure each person fills in at least one card.

2. **Draw cards.** Mix up the cards participants made with the ones you prepared ahead of time. Invite everyone to come up and draw a card. For this activity, small children need a reading partner who is not in her family. Partners can be older kids, teens, or other adults. The partners should also draw cards and participate.

3. **Swap cards.** Explain this part of the activity. **I'm going to play some music. As long as the music is playing, walk around and see what ideas are on the cards that other people have. If you see an idea that you like better than the one you have in your hand, trade. The person**

must trade (although be careful not to upset small children). **Then keep on walking around and swapping cards. As long as the music is playing, you may not sit down and you must let people see your cards.** Play some lively music for several minutes and give everyone a chance to swap cards several times.

4. **See what you have.** Invite everyone to read the ideas on their cards. If you have time, let people say why they liked the idea enough to take the card.

5. **Gather families.** Have families gather with all their members and talk about each idea. Is this an idea the family would like to try? When could they do this? What supplies do they need to gather? Distribute copies of the Family Night Planner on page 91 and give families time to fill out the page together. The challenge is to plan six family activities to enjoy together over the next few weeks. Families are not limited to the cards they hold. They can use any ideas they heard that interested them or think of on their own. If some individuals don't have families present, connect them to family units as honorary members or see if they'd like to form a group of their own.

6. **Gather your whole group.** Enjoy the Take It Home time together.

> ### Family Connections
> - Parents find out what kids are interested in.
> - Families practice talking and planning together.
> - Kids have a voice in what the family chooses to do.

Take It Home

> **Bible Verse:** "As for me and my household, we will serve the Lord" (Joshua 24:15).

Go around the group and give each family an opportunity to share one of the ideas they chose to use.

Families are great. Families are people who love us no matter what, the people we can always go home to. Not every family has a mom and dad and kids, but every family can love each other and spend time together doing things they enjoy.

Joshua was a leader of the people in Israel in Bible times. He wanted to make sure that the families of Israel would serve the Lord together. He reminded the people of everything God had done for them, bringing them out of slavery in Egypt and into the new land that God gave them. Joshua said that families could choose whom they wanted to serve, then he said, "But as for me and my household, we will serve the Lord."

Ask: **How can families serve the Lord together?** Ask: **Why is it important for us to choose to serve the Lord?**

One of the ways families can serve the Lord is by being healthy, loving families. The plans you made today for how to spend time together will help you do that.

Close with a prayer asking God to bless the families and individuals in your congregation.

Family Night Planner

We love to spend time together!
Here are a few of our favorite ways.

Our Idea:	Our Idea:	Our Idea:
When:	When:	When:
What we need:	What we need:	What we need:

Our Idea:	Our Idea:	Our Idea:
When:	When:	When:
What we need:	What we need:	What we need:

If you have more great ideas, ask for another copy of the Family Night Planner or write on the back of this page.

Copyright © 2007 by Susan Martins Miller. Permission is granted to reproduce this page for ministry purposes only—not for resale.

I'll-Remember-You Quilt

Many children have a favorite blanket or quilt. Even older kids or teenagers remember the blankets they loved so much when they were younger. A quilt carries memories and warmth and comfort. Participants of all ages will recognize that the gift of a quilt will speak volumes of love. Use the I'll Remember Quilt project to say farewell to a beloved family moving away, to comfort someone in a difficult time, or to simply say "We love you."

Set It Up

Supplies:

- fabric according to selected quilt design
- matching colored thread
- measuring tape
- scissors
- quilt batting
- sewing machines and operators
- quilting pins
- fabric markers or fabric paints (for Option 1)

Optional:

- flat sheet for backing

Do Ahead ≫ You can put together an I'll-Remember-You Quilt several ways. You might have a night where individuals and families prepare blocks and then assemble them on another occasion. The sewing involved in these quilts is not difficult. You might prefer to have quilters in your congregation put the blocks together and bring back the finished project. It makes a great mentoring project between quilters and those who want to learn. Choose your approach and decide what do-ahead steps make sense for you.

Option! ≫ A small group can make either of these quilts in one day (except hand quilting).

Get It Done

1. **Make the quilt top.** Option 1 is the easiest option. Each family or individual who wants to participate gets a blank block of white fabric all cut to the same size. If you meet together, they can use fabric markers or fabric paint to design a block and sign it. You might prefer to distribute blocks for people to finish at home in any way they wish—cross stitching, embroidery, appliqué, or fabric markers. Children can easily participate in a fabric marker design. Then collect the blocks to assemble. Cut strips of a coordinating fabric to put between blocks and to create a border. (See the diagram on page 94.) You can make the quilt any size you like by simply adding blocks.

   Option 2 is a bit more complicated but still fairly simple. It will involve selecting four different fabrics and cutting squares and rectangles and sewing them together according to the pattern and instructions on page 95. The instructions are for a twin size quilt. You can enlarge your quilt by adding another set of blocks to each row and by increasing the number of rows.

2. **Add the batting and backing.** Batting comes in prepackaged sizes that match various bed sizes, or you can buy it by the yard off a large roll in a fabric store. You can make the quilt backing from lengths of fabric of your choice sewn together. Using a flat sheet is an easy option because it is all in one piece without seams. Lay the backing out in your work space. You'll probably need to use the floor. Then add the batting layer. The batting should be a few inches larger than the quilt top all the way around. Finally lay out the completed quilt top. Starting at the center, make sure to smooth out any wrinkles or unintended folds in the backing or top. Use quilting pins at frequent intervals to hold the layers together.

3. **Tie or quilt the layers.** A quick option for holding the quilt together is to tie it together at the block corners. Choose a matching shade of yarn and use a large needle to thread the yarn down through the layers and back up again. Tie securely on the top layer. If you have people in your congregation who are skilled at machine quilting or hand quilting, and you have the time available, you may choose one of these options.

4. **Add the border.** Cut lengths of fabric in any width you like from four inches wide to ten inches wide. Stitch lengths together to match the length and width of the quilt. Lay a border length face down along the edge of the quilt top and stitch through all layers. Wrap the border around to the back of the quilt and hand stitch in place.

Family Connections

- Kids share in memories.
- Kids and parents meet a challenge together.
- Kids see how far the faith family extends.

5. **Share memories and purpose for making the quilt.** Make sure everyone knows whom the quilt is for and why. As you work together, also bond together in love for the quilt recipient. Consider finding a Bible verse that is particularly meaningful to your situation and including it with the quilt.

Quilt Layout

Follow this basic layout to create a memory quilt of blocks that individuals and families create. Have a quilting team add the backing, batting, and binding. Be sure to pre-wash all fabric.

Copyright © 2007 by Susan Martins Miller. Permission is granted to reproduce this page for ministry purposes only—not for resale.

Quilt, Option 2

1. Choose four fabrics and purchase 1 1/2 yards of each. Prewash.
2. Cut the fabrics into strips 8 1/2″ wide.
3. Two fabrics will be rectangles. Cut the strips of these fabrics into rectangles that are 4 1/2″ x 8 1/2″.
4. Two fabrics will be squares. Cut the strips of these fabrics into squares that are 4 1/2″ x 4 1/2″.
5. Stitch squares and rectangles together one row at a time, following the pattern below. You can pin the pieces together (right sides together) before sewing if that helps you keep things in order.
6. As each row is completed, stitch it to the previous row, being careful to match up corners as closely as possible.

Copyright © 2007 by Susan Martins Miller. Permission is granted to reproduce this page for ministry purposes only—not for resale.

Sassy Summer Bash

Summer is finally here! In some parts of the country, winter seems to last forever. When summer arrives, people want to take advantage of every moment. Plan a time for your faith family to enjoy an outdoor summer blast of games and ice cream.

Set It Up

Supplies:

- items for selected games (See pages 98 and 99.)
- ice cream
- ice cream toppings (syrups, colorful candies, marshmallows, whipped cream, cherries, bananas, nuts, sprinkles, etc.)
- plastic bowls and spoons
- cold drinks and ice
- paper cups
- silly prizes
- water spray bottle or squirt gun

Optional:

- CD player and music CDs

Do Ahead ≫ Recruit volunteers to organize and run the games. Also arrange for a welcome team to let people know where everything is. Pour ice cream toppings into separate bowls. Set up any lawn games you decide to use. Put out cold drinks and cups. If you have a large CD player or small sound system, be ready to play some lively music.

Option! ≫ Crank homemade ice cream during the games.

Get It Done ≫ 1. **Set up the games.** Choose from the games on pages 98 and 99 or introduce some of your own. Try to have a mix of games: lively water games, team games, individual challenges, games suitable for younger kids, activities parents and kids can enjoy together, etc.

2. **Welcome participants.** As people arrive, let them know what the activity options are. You might want to have a couple of people to mix and mingle and make sure others engage in the activities.

3. **Announce the ice cream sundaes.** Let people know what time and where to gather for a Take It Home time and ice cream sundaes. Send around some older kids to remind people when the time is near.

4. **Gather your group.** Enjoy the Take It Home time together.

5. **Enjoy the ice cream.** For those who wish to participate, hold an ice cream sundae contest. Serve everyone two scoops of vanilla ice cream in bowls. Point out the ice cream sundae toppings and announce the contest categories, such as most colorful, most sloppy, most tidy, most appealing, or most humanlike. Give the contest players a set time to work on their creations, such as two minutes. Onlookers will vote for the winner in each category. Give some silly prizes. Then everyone can enjoy ice cream festivities.

6. **Clean up.** Make sure to arrange a clean-up crew to take down all the games. Don't forget that kids can help if you give them clear instructions about what needs to be done and how to do it. Kids need to know they can make a meaningful contribution to the life of the faith family.

Family Connections

- Kids and parents laugh and play together.
- Families and individuals share in the larger faith family.
- Kids and parents share challenges in a non-threatening environment.

Take It Home

> **Bible Verse:** "Light is shed upon the righteous and joy on the upright in heart" (Psalm 97:11).

Cheer if you love summer! Cheer if you love hot weather! Cheer if you love the sunshine!

Spray water over people in the front of your group. Don't be timid.

Ask: **What makes you glad that winter is over?** People might mention longer daylight, better weather, being out doors, etc.

Ask: **What's your favorite part of summer?** People might mention the warm weather, vacations, water sports, gardening, and so on.

Summer brings sunshine. Sometimes winter skies are so cloudy and gray that we feel like we don't see the sun for weeks. Then summer comes and we can't get enough of the sun. The days are longer; evenings are light enough to do things outside. We love it! Let's read a Bible verse about light.

Have a volunteer read Psalm 97:11 from a Bible. Ask: **How does this verse remind you of summer?** Light shines and we feel happy. Ask: **How does God shed His light on us?** By His grace, love, care for us, giving us what we need, giving us joy on the inside.

Spray more water—generously! **Every day that you're out in the summer sunshine, and maybe when you're getting a little wet, remember that God pours His light and joy on you.**

Lawn Games

- croquet
- volleyball
- badminton
- bocce ball

Apple on a Rope

Supplies: apples, thin rope

Pair up players and give each pair an apple on a rope. Poke a hole through the apple and string a length of rope about three feet long through the apple. Knot it several times at the end to keep the apple from sliding off. Each pair should choose an apple holder and an apple eater. Have the apple eaters sit down. The apple holders dangle the apple in front of the eaters. Eaters are not allowed to use their hands. The first player to eat the apple down to the core wins. Play several rounds.

Rubber Boot Toss

Supplies: child's rubber boot, sand, duct tape

Fill a child's boot with sand and duct tape the top closed. Have all players line up along a straight line. One player at a time will heave the boot as far as possible. Mark on the ground where the boot lands each time to see who can throw it the farthest.

Flour Cherry

Supplies: 5 lb. bag of flour, maraschino cherries, spatula, newspaper

Spread newspaper on a table. Pour out the entire bag of flour in a pile on the newspaper and scoop it into the tightest pile you can. Put a cherry at the top of the pile. Players take turns using a spatula to remove a scoop of flour. Anyone who causes the cherry to fall must pick it up with his or her teeth. No hands allowed. Put a new cherry on top of the pile and play again.

Guess That Smell

Supplies: film canisters with lids, cotton balls, various scents (peppermint, vanilla, garlic, orange, lemon, coffee, sodas, etc.)

Put a cotton ball in each film canister. Poke a small hole in each canister lid. Add a scent to each cotton ball. See who can guess the scent in each canister.

Mud Painting

Supplies: garden shovels, garden hose, old paintbrushes

Let kids have a blast digging a pile of dirt. Then add water to make mud. Take the mud to a hard surface such as a sidewalk or parking lot and let kids paint with the mud. Use the hose at full water pressure to clean off the surface.

Shower Curtain Turnover

Supplies: plastic shower curtains
You need 8 to 12 players for each shower curtain. Have everyone stand on the shower curtain. The challenge is to turn the shower curtain over completely—without anyone stepping off the curtain. All players must be standing on the curtain at all times. They may use their hands.

Soap Slide

Supplies: large plastic garbage bags, liquid dish soap, hose or sprinkler
Spread out the plastic on the lawn. Pour a small amount of dish soap on the plastic and turn on the hose. Kids love to run and slide, especially on a hill. You might want to cut open the bags to make a longer plastic surface.

Fruit and Vegetable Prints

Supplies: fruits and vegetables (apples, pears, potatoes), art paper, tempera paints, art paper
Cut the fruits and vegetables in half. If you want, trim away more on the outside to create a distinct shape on the cut end. Use the fruits and vegetables as stamps. Dip them in paint and stamp on paper.

Hacky Sack

Supplies: hacky sack or bean bag
Gather a circle of players, about six to eight people. Take turns kicking the hacky sack or beanbag around the circle. Try to get it all the way around the circle with no one dropping it.

Faith Family "Fotos"

Supplies: cameras
Put a team of older kids in charge of taking photographs of the summer bash for everyone to enjoy later.

Copyright © 2007 by Susan Martins Miller. Permission is granted to reproduce this page for ministry purposes only—not for resale.

Faith Foundations

On the next 12 pages, you'll find reproducible pages to copy and distribute to families. Decide how you want to use them. You could hand them out as people mingle after a worship service, send them home with kids, or mail them to homes of your congregation members. The 12 themes are:

You Are Valuable. *God treasures each person.*
God Loves You. *God gave His Son for us.*
Love the Bible. *God's Word is a guide for life.*
Pray with Confidence. *God listens and responds to our needs.*
Put Others First. *Jesus is an example of humility.*
Be Thankful. *We thank God for who He is, not just what He gives us.*
Praise God. *The Bible tells us over and over to praise God.*
Be Joyful. *Even when things look dark, God is our source of joy.*
Be Generous. *God wants us to give cheerfully.*
The Holy Spirit. *God gives His Spirit to help us know how to please Him.*
Serve God. *Follow Jesus' example of self-sacrifice.*
The Kingdom Is Forever. *We look forward to eternity with Jesus.*

Each Faith Foundation highlights a basic concept of faith with these three elements:

God's Word Says:
Parents can read the Bible verse ahead of time.

We Believe:
Parents get some quick thoughts about what the verse means for personal faith. They may want to work these thoughts into a conversation with their kids.

Faith in Action:
This is a brief devotional time the family can enjoy together. It's not meant to be long or complicated, but rather something straightforward and short, so parents can feel successful at creating meaningful family time. It's interactive so everyone can participate.

Use these Faith Foundation reproducible pages to help parents explore some basic discipleship concepts with their kids.

You Are Valuable

God's Word Says:

"Are not two sparrows sold for a penny? Yet not one of them will fall to the ground apart from the will of your Father. And even the very hairs of your head are all numbered. So don't be afraid; you are worth more than many sparrows" (Matthew 10:29-31).

We Believe:

Sparrows are small, common birds. We don't think too much about them. But God does. Jesus said that not even a tiny sparrow is outside of God's care. If God cares that much about a bird, imagine how much more He cares about you. God created you in His image and wants to have a relationship with you. Even with six billion people on the planet, *you* are valuable to God.

Faith in Action:

1. Read Matthew 10:29-31 together. If you have very young children, you may want to find the passage in a children's Bible. Talk briefly about:

   • When you read these verses, what do you think God feels for you?
   • How does God show that you are valuable to Him?

2. Find a shoebox with a lid and cover the box and the lid with decorative paper. If possible, make it look like a treasure box. Try gold rickrack or ribbon and glitter glue. Ask everyone in the family to find something small that can remind all of you how valuable you are to God. Take turns telling why you picked the items you did. Put all the items in the treasure box. Choose a day in the future (such as in three months, or six months, or a holiday) to open the box and talk again about how valuable you are to God.

3. Pray a prayer like this one. *Lord, You care about the smallest sparrow! Sometimes we feel as small and weak as a sparrow. It's good to remember how much You love and value us. Thank You for keeping us in your treasure chest. Amen.*

Copyright © 2007 by Susan Martins Miller. Permission is granted to reproduce this page for ministry purposes only—not for resale.

God Loves You

God's Word Says:

"For God so loved the world that he gave his one and only Son, that whoever believes in him shall not perish but have eternal life" (John 3:16).

We Believe:

John 3:16 is one of the first Bible verses children learn because it's such a great summary of why Jesus came to die for us. Parents can't begin to imagine what it would be like to willingly sacrifice a child for any reason. It's too horrible to think about. But that's what God did—gave His Son to die for sinful humans so that these same humans could live with God forever. Jesus took the punishment that we deserved.

Faith in Action:

1. Read John 3:16 together. If you have young children, you might want to find the verse in a children's Bible. Talk briefly about:

   - Why did God give us His Son?
   - When you think about how much God loves you, how does that make you feel?

2. Fold a piece of poster board in half. If you don't have poster board, tape together two large pieces of construction paper so they open like a card. On the front of the card write in large letters "I love you." Inside the card, write "From, God." Use markers to draw a picture of a cross in the card to remind you that Jesus died for you. Glue pictures of the people in your family around the cross. If you'd like, glue pictures of extended family and friends in the card as a reminder that Jesus loves and died for everyone in the world.

3. Pray a prayer like this one: *Lord Jesus, You gave Your life to show us how much You love us. We love You too! Help us find ways to show our love for You every day. In Your name, amen.*

Copyright © 2007 by Susan Martins Miller. Permission is granted to reproduce this page for ministry purposes only—not for resale.

Love the Bible

God's Word Says:

"How sweet are your words to my taste, sweeter than honey to my mouth!" (Psalm 119:103).

We Believe:

The words in the Bible are not just words; they are God's Word—what God wants to say to us. God inspired humans to write the words of the Bible so that we would have God's Word. The Bible helps us to know God better and how to be more like Him. It helps us know what choices please Him, and it tells the great story of what God has done for us so that we can live with Him forever.

Faith in Action:

1. Read Psalm 119:103 together. If you have young children, you might want to find the verse in a children's Bible. Put a small amount of honey in a bowl and taste it with your fingers while you talk about:

   • How can words be sweet like honey?
   • How is God's Word sweet in your life?

2. Get out index cards or small squares of paper, markers, and Bibles. Choose Bible verses that you'd like to memorize together as a family. Copy the verses on index cards. Plan to learn a new verse each week. Let the youngest member of the family choose which verse to learn first. Work on it whenever you sit down together for a meal. When everyone can say the first verse without looking at the words, choose another verse to work on.

3. Pray a prayer like this one: *Heavenly Father, You tell us so much about yourself in Your Word. Help us to show our love for You by loving Your Word and making it a part of our lives. In Jesus' name, amen.*

Copyright © 2007 by Susan Martins Miller. Permission is granted to reproduce this page for ministry purposes only—not for resale.

Pray with Confidence

God's Word Says:

"Do not be anxious about anything, but in everything, by prayer and petition, with thanksgiving, present your requests to God" (Philippians 4:6).

We Believe:

God cares what happens to us. He wants us to talk to him about what we need and the things that make us worried. We can tell him everything and ask him for anything. And we can always be thankful because we know how much He cares about us. God wants us to rest in His care, rather than wasting energy being anxious. We can pray with confidence that God is listening.

Faith in Action:

1. Read Philippians 4:6 together. If you have young children, you might want to find the verse in a children's Bible. Talk briefly about:

   - What kinds of things make you worry?
   - How can prayer help you not worry?

2. Find a fancy sheet of paper and a nice pen. Gather the family and write a list of things to pray about together. You can pray about anything that's on your minds. God cares about everything that happens to you. Leave space between the items on your list. If you'd like, make a colorful border around the page or write a favorite Bible verse somewhere on the page. Each evening before bedtime, choose a new item on the list and pray for God's help and presence in that situation. As you see God answer your prayers, write about the answers in the spaces you left on your prayer list.

3. Pray a prayer like this one: *Heavenly Father, thank You that You care about everything that happens to us. Help us to bring our worries to You and be confident that You will do what's best. In Jesus' name, amen.*

Copyright © 2007 by Susan Martins Miller. Permission is granted to reproduce this page for ministry purposes only—not for resale.

Put Others First

God's Word Says:

"Be devoted to one another in brotherly love. Honor one another above yourselves" (Romans 12:10).

We Believe:

Jesus is the ultimate example of humble self-sacrifice. Even though He is God, He came to earth as a human being and even gave His life for us. He wasn't thinking of himself; He was thinking of us. He gave our need more priority that what He himself deserved. God tells us to follow Jesus' example and be ready to put others first, thinking about what others need instead of just what we want for ourselves.

Faith in Action:

1. Read Romans 12:10 together. If you have young children, you might want to find the verse in a children's Bible. Talk briefly about:

   • What does it mean to be devoted to each other?
   • Name some ways you can honor each other in your family.

2. Cut some construction paper into squares. Have each family member choose a color and make a stack of squares. On each square, write "You're #1." Discuss ways that you can put each other first in everyday situations, such as who gets to choose the first piece of cake or choose a board game to play or go first down the slide. Here's your assignment for the week: When you want to put someone else first, give that person one of your #1 cards. See how long it takes for each one to give away her cards.

3. Pray a prayer like this one: *Lord Jesus, we can put others first because You showed us how when You put us first. Be with us at times when we want our own way and help us to put others first. In Your name, amen.*

Copyright © 2007 by Susan Martins Miller. Permission is granted to reproduce this page for ministry purposes only—not for resale.

Be Thankful

God's Word Says:

"Give thanks to the Lord, for he is good. His love endures forever" (Psalm 136:1).

We Believe:

We don't thank God just for what He gives us or what He does for us. We thank Him because He is good. That's His character. He's not good just when He feels like it, like when children behave well or when adults give their best effort. God is good. Always. He shows His love to us every day in new ways. Whether the circumstances of our lives are fantastic or miserable, we give thanks to God because He is good.

Faith in Action:

1. Read Psalm 136:1 together. If you have young children, you might want to find the verse in a children's Bible. Talk briefly about:

   • Name some ways that God is good to you.
   • Name some ways that you can show your gratitude to God.

2. Get out a piece of poster board, magazines, family photos, scissors, glue, and markers. Make a collage of things you are thankful for—ways that God has shown His goodness in your life. You can use pictures from magazines, family photos, or your own drawings. When the collage is finished, look at it to see what everyone added. Show God your thankfulness with a simple sentence and response. Have one person say, "Lord, we thank You for _____." Fill in the blank with one of the items from the collage. Then the rest of the family answers, "His love endures forever."

3. Pray a prayer like this one: *Thank You, Lord, for Your love. Thank You for Your goodness. Thank You for caring for us every day in any situation. Your love is forever. Help us to show our thankfulness in ways that please You. In Your name, amen.*

Copyright © 2007 by Susan Martins Miller. Permission is granted to reproduce this page for ministry purposes only—not for resale.

Praise God

God's Word Says:

"I will praise you as long as I live, and in your name I will lift up my hands" (Psalm 63:4).

We Believe:

The Bible tells us over and over to praise God—at home, in the streets, in worship, in private, in public, in song, with instruments, in times of joy, and in times of sorrow. Praise should be at the core of our lives. And praise is the antidote to many heavy hearts. When we praise God, we take our eyes off our own troubles and lift them to God's greatness.

Faith in Action:

1. Read Psalm 63:4 together. If you have young children, you might want to find the verse in a children's Bible. Talk briefly about:

   • Take turns naming things for which we can praise God.
   • How does praising God make you feel?

2. Have everyone in the family choose a favorite praise song and sing it. For a little extra fun, put together a kitchen band. Bang some pots, find something to twang, blow over a jug filled with water, or shake a container of beans. Scrounge around the kitchen and be creative until everyone has something to blow, drum, or shake. Add your instruments to your praise songs and make a joyful noise!

3. Pray a prayer like this one: *Lord, You are so great. We can never find enough words and songs for the praise that You deserve. Help us to live lives of praise, showing honor to Your name in everything we do.*

Copyright © 2007 by Susan Martins Miller. Permission is granted to reproduce this page for ministry purposes only—not for resale.

Be Joyful

God's Word Says:

"Shout for joy to the Lord, all the earth. Worship the Lord with gladness; come before him with joyful songs" (Psalm 100:1, 2).

We Believe:

God is the source of joy. When God is in our lives, He gives a deep joy that undergirds our whole existence. This kind of joy is not about what makes us happy or how we show we're happy. It's deep down, and circumstances can't change it. The Bible says the joy of the Lord is our strength. It's our foundation, no matter what life brings.

Faith in Action:

1. Read Psalm 100:1, 2 together. If you have young children, you might want to find the verses in a children's Bible. Talk briefly about:

   • What kinds of things make you want to shout for joy?
   • How does joy help you when you're having a tough time?

2. The book of Psalms is full of expressions of praise and joy. Sometimes good things happen. Sometimes bad things happen. But with God's joy deep inside us, we can worship with gladness no matter what. Read these verses from the Psalms: Psalm 5:11; 28:7; 66:1; 90:14; 95:1; and 126:2. Talk about the verses together, and then write a family definition of joy.

3. Pray a prayer like this one: *Lord, You are the source of joy. Your joy is deep inside us. It carries us through good times and bad times. It bubbles up inside us and we can't help being glad. Thank You for putting Your joy in our hearts. Amen.*

Copyright © 2007 by Susan Martins Miller. Permission is granted to reproduce this page for ministry purposes only—not for resale.

Be Generous

God's Word Says:

"Remember this: Whoever sows sparingly will also reap sparingly, and whoever sows generously will also reap generously. Each man should give what he has decided in his heart to give, not reluctantly, or under compulsion, for God loves a cheerful giver" (2 Corinthians 9:6).

We Believe:

Sometimes we worry about whether we have enough money for our needs, so we hesitate to give to anyone else. This verse reminds us that God is able to meet all our needs. Don't let lack of faith keep you from being generous with others. Share your money, your time, your material possessions and your talents freely with others. God will give you what you need.

Faith in Action:

1. Read 2 Corinthians 9:6 together. If you have younger children, you might want to find the verse in a children's Bible. Talk briefly about:

   - What things does God give us every day that we don't always think about?
   - How do you feel on the inside when you share generously?

2. Find a medium or large box and fill it with items to give away. You can give items to people you know who need them or to an organization like Goodwill that helps families in need. Send everyone in the family on a treasure hunt and call everyone back together in five minutes to see what each one chose to give away. Here's the catch. Don't just choose things that don't fit or you don't use any more. Put things in the box that you do still enjoy because you know that someone else would enjoy them too. Ask family members to say why they want to be generous with the items they chose. Talk about what it means to be a cheerful giver.

3. Pray a prayer like this one: *Lord, we know that You can give us everything we need. Help us to trust You for what we need and share with others everything You give us. In Jesus' name, amen.*

Copyright © 2007 by Susan Martins Miller. Permission is granted to reproduce this page for ministry purposes only—not for resale.

The Holy Spirit

God's Word Says:

"Since we live by the Spirit, let us keep in step with the Spirit" (Galatians 5:25).

We Believe:

When we come to faith in Christ, we receive the Holy Spirit, who dwells within us. The Holy Spirit transforms us to be more and more like Jesus every day. Our sinful nature still calls to us, but now we have the Holy Spirit to help us step off the old path and step onto the new path—the path of discipleship. Since we have the Spirit, we can live the way the Spirit calls us to live.

Faith in Action:

1. Read Galatians 5:25 together. If you have young children, you might want to find the verse in a children's Bible. Talk briefly about:

   - What does it mean to keep in step with something?
   - How do we know we're keeping in step with the Holy Spirit?

2. Line up everybody in a straight line. Choose one person to be the "step leader." This person chooses a way to step across the room, and everyone else has to keep in step. Keep taking turns choosing how to step. Take a rest and review the words of Galatians 5:25. Take some more turns stepping, and this time say the words of the verse in step with each other.

3. Pray a prayer like this one: *Lord, we want to walk on the path You lead us on. Show us how to follow You, step by step. Help us to live in Your Spirit every day, in every way. In Jesus' name, amen.*

Copyright © 2007 by Susan Martins Miller. Permission is granted to reproduce this page for ministry purposes only—not for resale.

Serve God

God's Word Says:

"Serve wholeheartedly, as if you were serving the Lord, not men" (Ephesians 6:7).

We Believe:

Jesus gave us an example of self-sacrificing service to others. We can go through the motions of serving others. We can do all the right things and say all the right words. But that's not enough. God wants us to serve others wholeheartedly, with the right motivations and attitudes. He asks us to serve others just as if we were serving Him—and giving our best.

Faith in Action:

1. Read Ephesians 6:7 together. If you have young children, you might want to find the verse in a children's Bible. Talk briefly about:

   • What's the difference between "halfhearted" and "wholehearted"?
   • Name some people your family knows who you could serve together.

2. Plan a family service project. Decide whom you want to serve, what you want to do, and when you will do it. Give everyone a job for getting ready to serve together. Think of your own idea for a service project or use one of these: make and send cards to elderly people in your church who can't come to church very often; organize a food or clothing drive in your neighborhood and donate what you collect to an organization that serves needy people in your community; choose a park and clean it up together; clean and repair all the toys in the church nursery; contact a nursing home about a resident you can adopt and visit on a regular basis; make cookies, wrap up a dozen for each of your neighbors and deliver them with a cheery note; bake bread and deliver it to families who visit your church.

3. Pray a prayer like this one: *Lord, sometimes it's hard to stop thinking about what we want so we can serve others. Open our eyes. Show us the people around us who need to know You, and help us to show Your love by serving them. In Jesus' name, amen.*

Copyright © 2007 by Susan Martins Miller. Permission is granted to reproduce this page for ministry purposes only—not for resale.

The Kingdom Is Forever

God's Word Says:

"The seventh angel sounded his trumpet, and there were loud voices in heaven, which said: 'The kingdom of the world has become the kingdom of our Lord and of his Christ, and he will reign for ever and ever'" (Revelation 11:15).

We Believe:

When Jesus came to earth, He brought the kingdom of God. He called people to repent and be part of God's everlasting kingdom through a life of faith and discipleship. One day Jesus will come again, and the entire world will bow to Him and acknowledge Him as Lord. God's kingdom will have no end.

Faith in Action:

1. Read Revelation 11:15 together. If you have young children, you might want to find the verse in a children's Bible. Talk briefly about:

   - What do you think the "kingdom of our Lord" is like?
   - Use your own words to explain what "forever and ever" means.

2. Talk about time and what forever means. Start by having everyone in the family do a simple task or silly motion for 30 seconds. Then do something for one minute, then three minutes. Ask your children to tell you about how they know that years are passing, such as beginning a new grade or celebrating another Christmas. Think about experiences they are looking forward to in the future, such as learning to drive, going to college, getting married. Talk about how old each member of your family will be at a year in the future. Imagine what it would be like to live for 100 years, or even 200. How much will the world change in that time? Then imagine what it will be like to live forever in the kingdom of God. Share what you think Heaven will be like.

3. Pray a prayer like this one: *Lord, You are the almighty king of the universe. No one is greater than You are. Your kingdom is going to last forever, and we're so glad that You want us to be a part of it. Amen.*

Copyright © 2007 by Susan Martins Miller. Permission is granted to reproduce this page for ministry purposes only—not for resale.

Copy and Paste!

Do you ever wish you could touch the lives of your families more often than just when they come to church or attend special events? Give them something to chew on between church activities? Let parents know you understand the challenges they face on a daily basis? Remind them that God cares when they're overwhelmed or confused?

You can!

The following pages have brief articles related to child development and family living. Photocopy them into a format that works in your ministry setting. This may be a:

- bulletin insert,
- monthly church newsletter,
- special mailing, or
- handout to give parents when they pick up their kids.

Use the articles in any format that works for you. Choose the ones that most closely match the needs of your family and use them in any order.

There's Smart, and Then There's Smart

Some kids learn to read early, or are adept at math. They bring home good grades and memorize easily. But "school smart" is not the only kind of smart.

Kids are smart in several ways—and so are adults. *Word-smart* kids like words and ways to use them. *Music-smart* kids like rhythm and patterns in sound. *Logic-smart* kids enjoy figuring things out and have fun with science and riddles. *Picture-smart* kids love to look around and see all the interesting things in the world.

Body-smart kids are graceful and comfortable in their bodies. *People-smart* kids love interacting with other people. *Self-smart* kids understand themselves and their feelings. *Nature-smart* kids love being outdoors and notice plants, animals, and rocks.

Sometimes kids who don't quite fit in the traditional school system think they're not smart. But they are. Smart comes in many shapes and sizes, and everyone is smart in several ways. The various kinds of smarts work together, and no kind of smart is better than the others. Make sure your kids know that.

Make sure your kids know that you value the kind of smarts they have—even if it's not the same kind of smarts you have. Make sure your kids know that God created them and gave them gifts and personality. He treasures them just the way they are.

"You created my inmost being; you knit me together in my mother's womb. I praise you because I am fearfully and wonderfully made" (Psalm 139:13, 14).

Copyright © 2007 by Susan Martins Miller. Permission is granted to reproduce this page for ministry purposes only—not for resale.

Things Are Looking Up

Kids are born optimistic. They just are. So how come so many of them end up disgruntled, disappointed in themselves, even depressed? Sadly, sometimes parents pull the optimism rug out from under their own kids. We don't mean to. Most of the time we don't realize we're doing it.

It all comes down to talk. If we tell them they can be star soccer players when they know they can't run as fast as the other kids, maybe we're not helping all that much. What if they get out on the field and they are yards behind the pack—game after game? Now they're questioning our grip on reality or telling themselves they're failures because they can't do what we said they could do. Hopelessness and helplessness set in.

Now, don't think you can never encourage a child to keep trying or to pursue a goal. Just be straightforward about cause and effect. Some things take work; they don't happen just because you want them to. Help your kids learn to tell themselves the truth: "I don't run as fast as the other kids, but I'm a great blocker." "Reading is hard for me, but I'm the best math student in the class."

When kids know the truth, they have hope. As long as they have hope, they can keep depression at bay. Be intentional about the way you talk to your kids so they'll learn the right way to talk to themselves.

"But you have been my hope, O Sovereign Lord, my confidence since my youth" (Psalm 71:5)

Copyright © 2007 by Susan Martins Miller. Permission is granted to reproduce this page for ministry purposes only—not for resale.

Through a Toddler's Eyes

Surely you've noticed that your 2-year-old thinks the world exists to serve him. So what if another child is playing with that toy? So what if Mommy is talking on the phone? As a matter of fact, that's the way God wants toddlers to develop. That solid sense of self that comes by staking out territory in the toddler years is supposed to last a lifetime.

Parents gently help toddlers hang onto a sense of self while they learn that other people have feelings as well. We teach them to say "Sorry" and "Please" and "Thank you." We teach them to share and to give. All these things lay foundations for faith to grow in little ones. The caring, nurturing, personal relationships toddlers have prepare them for a caring, nurturing, personal relationship with God.

Toddler brains process experiences at an incredible rate. They're putting the pieces together constantly, exploring, experimenting, and logging the results in their brains. Kids learn about Jesus the same way—through experiences. Kids don't reach a certain age and suddenly understand theology. As they grow and learn new information, they reach back into the data bank and connect the new with something old.

So don't think a 2-year-old is too young to start learning about Jesus. Developing relationships with people they trust will help them someday to trust Jesus. Thriving in your love now will someday help them to thrive in God's love.

"Let the little children come to me" (Matthew 19:14).

Copyright © 2007 by Susan Martins Miller. Permission is granted to reproduce this page for ministry purposes only—not for resale.

Through a Preschooler's Eyes

To preschoolers, the world is a big place. They see a lot of kneecaps and thighs, and the most interesting things seem to be chronically out of reach. Their brains are in a perpetual high gear as language mushrooms and everything is a question they can't wait to ask. They're wiggly and squiggly, and swing from limitless energy to instant exhaustion. Laughter suddenly becomes tears, and they can't tell you why.

Is it hard? Is it heavy? Will it make a sound? What if I throw it? Preschoolers are constantly learning, and they learn through their senses. Activity is not optional—it's mandatory because if they're not moving and feeling and looking, they're not learning. What looks perfectly ordinary to adults is an adventure to preschoolers.

Sometimes it may seem as if it's all you can do to keep your child under control. Kids do need structure, but they need room to learn and grow, and you can help them. Provide an environment where it is safe for them to explore God's world, and talk about the God who created everything. Join them in their sense of wonder, rather than take the ordinary for granted. Help preschoolers find words for their emotions, and talk about God's love for them. Foster their rapidly expanding language with the adventures you find in the Bible. Read a Bible story, and then let little ones tell it back to you.

Preschoolers can't understand theology, but they can understand that Jesus loves them. At this stage in their development, children accept what the people caring for them tell them. So take advantage of the many moments every day that you can share the truth of God in the ways that matter most to them.

"At that time Jesus said, 'I praise you, Father, Lord of heaven and earth, because you have hidden these things from the wise and learned, and revealed them to little children'" (Matthew 11:25).

Copyright © 2007 by Susan Martins Miller. Permission is granted to reproduce this page for ministry purposes only—not for resale.

Early Elementary Eyes

Young children believe everything you tell them. If you're doing your job as a parent in caring for your kids, why would they have reason to doubt? Then the world breaks in and kids in the early elementary years discover not everything is true. Kids make fun of other kids. People deceive each other. Words have hidden meanings. Even grown-ups can be cruel.

Enter right and wrong. Of course, right and wrong have always existed, but up until now, your kids trusted you to help them know the difference. Now they've reached an age where they begin to evaluate situations on their own, decide what's right or wrong, and act on it. Sometimes they make a not-so-good choice. Sometimes they experiment to see what happens if they do something they know is wrong. Talk about conscience and consequences. Provide firm guidance to get them back on track—but this time of their own will.

Kids this age are eager to learn about God. As they discriminate between fact and fantasy, they know that Jesus is not in the same category as the Easter Bunny. They love Bible stories, especially as they learn to read for themselves. Praying seems natural. Take advantage of this important window in your child's developing faith. Just as they learn to choose right and wrong for themselves, they can choose Jesus for themselves. As they become aware of their own sin, they become aware that they need Jesus.

"My son, do not forget my teaching, but keep my commands in your heart" (Proverbs 3:1).

Coptright © 2007 by Susan Martins Miller. Permission is granted to reproduce this page for ministry purposes only—not for resale.

Upper Elementary Eyes

Remember play dates? When you chose who your child played with and when and where? Those days are gone when kids hit the upper elementary years. Kids this age choose a lot more things for themselves. Sometimes they choose well, sometimes not so well. Parents want to step in and put kids back on the clear path. Sometimes, though, the best thing to do is step aside and let kids experiences the consequences of their choices. Not everything in their whole lives will go right. Let them learn to grow even through failure within a safe, loving home.

As they learn to evaluate their own choices, upper elementary kids also evaluate what they think and believe. They begin to ask questions about the faith they've been learning at home and church. It might even seem like they've taken up debate as a new hobby! Relax. This is a normal phase of development. Kids this age can think more abstractly than younger kids, so their ideas get bigger and bigger. They're moving toward a more internal faith, one that applies to their own behavior and choices.

So stay close by, answer questions, admit you have questions of your own, join your kids in looking at a subject—even Christianity—from several angles. Be a safe place for kids to express their feelings. As kids realize the world is not perfect, and they're not perfect themselves, they'll see their need for God more and more.

"These commandments that I give you today are to be upon your hearts. Impress them on your children" (Deuteronomy 6:6, 7).

Copyright © 2007 by Susan Martins Miller. Permission is granted to reproduce this page for ministry purposes only—not for resale.

The Young Teen Puzzle

You may be raising the next SAT genius, or you may live with someone who fervently believes rules are made to be broken. Either way, what you have on your hands is a teenager trying to figure out who she is. Adolescence is about finding your identity. "What do you want to be when you grow up?" gets frighteningly real.

In the process of finding answers to identity questions, interests change. She used to cry when she missed a dance lesson; now she likes to watch old movies. He used to beg to go to the batting cages; now lacrosse is the only thing that matters. Take a breath and step back. These shifts are normal. She may come back to dance, and he may go back to the batting cages, but right now they're looking around to see what else is out there. Supporting your kids during this explora-tion period affirms their value.

Adolescence is also the time for kids to develop a worldview, although they won't call it that. Exploration leads to lasting values that they begin to put into action. This may be the time when they get serious about faith. Parents get a little nervous if teens explore too much outside familiar faith boundaries. Remind yourself that you've laid the foundation and now it's time for your son or daughter to take ownership. In the meantime, keep your own relationship with God on track.

"You will keep in perfect peace him whose mind is steadfast, because he trusts in you" (Isaiah 26:3).

Copyright © 2007 by Susan Martins Miller. Permission is granted to reproduce this page for ministry purposes only—not for resale.

Your Faith in Your Child

Children love to learn about God. They learn about someone who loves them immensely and can solve any problem. The stories are great! Younger kids believe what you tell them, and they want to be like you. They're happy to fold their hands and pray and sing songs about Jesus. It's normal for kids to mimic the adults in their lives, especially the ones closest to them.

Elementary age kids love to hear stories of when their parents were children. When you tell the stories, you share what's important in your life—what you value, what you believe, the foundations of your faith. By the time they're teenagers, kids know what their parents believe and are sorting out for themselves what they believe.

Your kids are watching your faith, trying it out. They watch how you respond to stress or to bad news or a new challenge or a strained relationship or a financial crisis. Do you pray? Do you ask God what to do? Do you answer God's call? Do you take the first step to forgive? Do you give generously when it seems you have nothing to give?

Passing on your faith is not about telling Bible stories and imparting flawless doctrine. It's showing kids how to be more like Jesus every day, in any situation, in every situation. Put your faith to work so your kids can see what God can do.

"By faith we eagerly await through the Spirit the righteousness for which we hope" (Galatians 5:5).

Copyright © 2007 by Susan Martins Miller. Permission is granted to reproduce this page for ministry purposes only—not for resale.

Will You Please Stop Fighting?

Moooom! Daaaad! You groan because you know what's coming next. They expect you to arbitrate. Whatever you say, one child will gloat and the other will protest the injustice.

Siblings fight for lots of reasons. They may be competing for your attention—and even negative attention from you is attention. They may be aware of differences between them—what they have, what they can do—and these differences become a source of friction. An older child may bellow when a younger sibling invades the privacy of the older one. They may harass each other in constant power plays.

What's a parent to do? First of all, remember that most sibling rivalry has nothing to do with poor parenting, so don't waste a lot of time wondering what you've done wrong that you've raised such combative children. Try not to get sucked into every dispute—especially if you think the dispute may be a misguided plea for your attention. Discourage tattling and be consistent in conveying the standards of behavior you expect. However, don't turn your back completely. Kids usually will work out more than we give them credit for, but conflicts can get out of hand, and you need to be ready to step in when they do. Don't let someone get hurt.

It's a phase, and it will pass. Often kids who squabbled the most are fiercely fond and loyal to each other as adults.

"Be devoted to one another in brotherly love. Honor one another above yourselves" (Romans 12:10).

Copyright © 2007 by Susan Martins Miller. Permission is granted to reproduce this page for ministry purposes only—not for resale.

Kids and Iron Will

"You can't make me!" Oooh. Them's fightin' words. When they come out of a child and are aimed at you, you may get your back up with good reason. You are the parent, after all.

Therein lies the danger. You are the parent. This child should respect your authority. This child should do as you ask. This child should take responsibility. All true. But do you really want to make every issue a power struggle? What's the larger goal? What's the best way to motivate this child in all those areas? It may not be by getting your back up, determined to win the power struggle.

A strong-willed child can argue the smallest point into the ground, or take something trivial and inflate it into a life issue. And when you appeal to reason or resort to threats, the child is ready to give up what he wants just so you don't get what you want. He can't play soccer unless he cleans his room. He shrugs. OK, no soccer.

No one will say it's easy, but try to keep a positive focus. As frustrating as this ironclad behavior is to you as a parent, it's not necessarily a negative trait in the grand scheme of things. Someday it may mature into determination, perseverance, persistence—traits essential to many of life's challenges and accomplishments. So rather than contributing to the deterioration of a power play, step back and reflect on the big picture of your child. Chances are you'll find a better motivator than "because I said so."

"I have chosen the way of truth; I have set my heart on your laws" (Psalm 119:30).

Copyright © 2007 by Susan Martins Miller. Permission is granted to reproduce this page for ministry purposes only—not for resale.

WHat Do YoU EXPect?

Why won't he do his homework before he turns on the TV? Why doesn't she stop grabbing things from her sister? Why are the dirty clothes everywhere except in the hamper?

What do you expect? Seriously, what do you expect? Have you communicated your expectation clearly, or have you just assumed that your child should know better? If you tell your daughter not to grab toys, your expectation probably is that she would find a more socially appropriate way to have a turn with a toy. So do you help her know how to ask?

Before you expect a certain behavior or response from your child, make sure you teach the behavior. Help your kids pick up their rooms and deliberately put the dirty clothes in the hamper. Next, make sure your child understands what you want. You can ask a direct question: What would I like you to do with your dirty clothes? Then make sure your child is able to do what you want—it's not too hard, not too tall, not too complex, not unreasonable for your child's age, and so on. Make sure your expectation is something your child really can do successfully.

Clear expectations provide the basic structure for the positive behavior we all want to see in our kids. Your kids won't meet your expectations perfectly every time. Think long term. Over time, your consistency and persistence will pay off.

"Train a child in the way he should go, and when he is old he will not turn from it" (Proverbs 22:6).

Copyright © 2007 by Susan Martins Miller. Permission is granted to reproduce this page for ministry purposes only—not for resale.

FirM and Fair

Little Isabel crawled toward the outlet, looking over her shoulder at her caregiver. Isabel knew the answer would be "no." Still she crawled, and tentatively lifted her hand, looking over her shoulder again.

Isabel wanted to know if the rule applied every time, or what would happen if she broke it. Kids of all ages need boundaries and structure. Love may be number one on the list of things kids need from their parents, but structure is probably number two.

Some parents hesitate to set limits. The parents themselves don't like to be told what to do, so they assume kids feel the same way. So why overdo it? Why not give kids free-range as much as possible?

Kids are not little adults. Structure and boundaries tell kids that parents care. They pro-vide patterns that help kids learn how to manage their own behavior and keep themselves safe. If parents don't provide the structure externally, kids have far more trouble developing the internal structure they need in their adult lives.

Realize that your child is changing and developing, growing from one stage to the next. Change the rules appropriately along the way. Gradually give more freedom to make choices—and accept the consequences. Be intentional about this process along the way, and the day will come when your child will set healthy boundaries on her own.

"I will instruct you and teach you in the way you should go; I will counsel you and watch over you" (Psalm 32:8).

Copyright © 2007 by Susan Martins Miller. Permission is granted to reproduce this page for ministry purposes only—not for resale.

Teachable Moments With Your Child

Sunday school is a great way to teach children about Jesus. Teachers use planned lessons about important concepts. But not every child is ready to learn at those moments. You're likely to be the one who's there when your child has a "teachable moment."

A teachable moment is a situation that comes up naturally and opens the door for you to talk to your child about something that may not be at the top of your child's interest list most of the time—but you know it's important. Taking advantage of a teachable moment means coming up with an informal lesson on the spot, when the situation arises. You don't know when it will be. But it doesn't have to be complicated.

Kids do and say things all the time that signal a curiosity or question they haven't verbalized.

When you're alert to recognize these moments, you can make the most of them. You're not sitting your child down for a structured Bible lesson or family devotions. You're responding to something that comes from your child and using the opportunity to share your values and your faith. You're listening and responding and engaging with your child, rather than just trying to keep him busy, or get done with the present task as quickly as you can.

Slow down. You don't want to miss these important moments in your child's life.

"Come, my children, listen to me. I will teach you the fear of the Lord" (Psalm 34:11).

Copyright © 2007 by Susan Martins Miller. Permission is granted to reproduce this page for ministry purposes only—not for resale.

What's Your Choice?

What decisions did your kids make today? Whether 3, 7, or 15, kids make decisions. How can you help them make good decisions?

Depending on the stage of development kids are in, they make decisions based on what they want for themselves at the moment, or strict adherence to black and white rules, or in a way that chooses the present over future consequences, whether good or bad.

You're not always there when your child makes a decision. But when you are, make the most of it. Help your child clarify what the question really is. Does she understand what she's choosing? Once you're sure she understands the question, go over the options. What will happen if she chooses this, or that? What are the advantages and disadvantages of each option?

Sometimes this process helps a child see that

the answer is not as obvious as he thought, and taking more time to decide is a good idea. Sometimes you may not agree with the final decision, such as the way your teenager spends money, but since it doesn't affect anyone but your child, you honor it. With older kids you can begin to talk about choices that honor God, which is the ultimate good decision.

As kids get older, they have to make more decisions more quickly. Practice with the small things, and they'll be ready when the big ones come along.

"Teach me your way, O Lord, and I will walk in your truth; give me an undivided heart, that I may fear your name" (Psalm 86:11).

Copyright © 2007 by Susan Martins Miller. Permission is granted to reproduce this page for ministry purposes only—not for resale.

What Kids Do to Parents

They were so cute when they were little. When did they become so conniving? How did they organize a union behind your back? Where did they get that secret play that always gets them what they want—and leaves you and your spouse in a spat?

The Bible tells us children are a blessing from the Lord. Life reminds us that they can take over the home pretty easily. The danger is that parents can be so absorbed in being parents that they have little energy left for being husbands or wives. Nearly every married person with kids can attest to the drain childrearing can be on marriage.

It's a mistake to take the marital relationship for granted, thinking that during the childrearing years the kids are what matters most. In between reading stories and playing sports and helping with homework and agonizing about teenage drivers, husbands and wives must remember each other. They were a family unit before the kids came along, and they'll be a family unit when the kids have moved out. They need to be a unit for the years in between.

And this is for the kids as much as it is for them. How does a boy learn to be a husband? How does a girl learn to be a wife? Ideally, from their own parents. Give them a good model. Communicate. Save some energy for each other. Carve out time to be together. Everybody—kids and parents—will benefit.

"For this reason a man will leave his father and mother and be united to his wife, and they will become one flesh" (Genesis 2:24).

Copyright © 2007 by Susan Martins Miller. Permission is granted to reproduce this page for ministry purposes only—not for resale.

Church and Home: Working Together

Church focuses on spiritual development of children. School focuses on mental development. Sports teams focus on physical development. Doesn't quite sound right, does it?

God didn't make kids in interchangeable pieces. Kids are whole human beings. They develop as whole human beings, not in fragments. So the faith journey is not something that happens only on Sundays. The faith journey is a life experience. Both church and home have a part.

God's plan for children's spiritual development includes a community of faith. In the Old Testament, family and community life centered around celebrating the great things God had done. Children were right there in the middle of the celebration. Parents were their primary teachers, and the classroom was the active, multi-sensory environment in which they lived. Whether they realize it or not, parents have far more influence on their children's developing faith than a teacher or church program does.

Church and home work together in a child's life. If kids see the truth of the Sunday school lesson at work in their parents, they'll believe it's true. When "love one another" seems abstract, parents can show how to put feet on the concept. When "forgive one another" seems impossible, what better demonstration than family relationships?

Parents and children's ministry workers share the goal of seeing kids develop personal relationships with Jesus and grow to be more and more like Him. It's not "either/or." It's "both/and." Both church and home.

"Speaking the truth in love, we will in all things grow up into him who is the Head, that is, Christ" (Ephesians 4:15).

Copyright © 2007 by Susan Martins Miller. Permission is granted to reproduce this page for ministry purposes only—not for resale.

Leading Your Child to Christ

The statistics are overwhelming—a large majority of Christians come to faith before the age of 14. And parents are the great spiritual influence on their kids. Whether you feel prepared or not, you're in a great position to help your child begin a personal relationship with Jesus and look forward to living with Jesus in Heaven.

You can begin praying for your child to come to faith before she is even born. You can be a consistent positive model of a life of faith. You can openly answer questions about the Bible and God. When the moment is right, you be ready to share specific verses with your child.

Psalm 139, especially verses 13-16, is a great passage to help kids understand how precious they are to God. Romans 3:23 tells them that everyone sins. Everyone messes up. We can't do everything right in our own strength. First John 1:9 assures us that if we confess our sin, God will always forgive. John 3:16 may already be a familiar verse to your child, but perhaps now is the time to look at it carefully and understand its meaning. Talk about what it means to believe in Jesus. Offer to pray with your child. And don't forget the end of the story—believers are children of God!

"How great is the love the Father has lavished on us, that we should be called children of God! And that is what we are!" (1 John 3:1).

Copyright © 2007 by Susan Martins Miller. Permission is granted to reproduce this page for ministry purposes only—not for resale.

Where Do I Fit In?

Your first child had you all to himself for four years before the next baby came along. Or your older daughter is pretty, friendly, and talented, and your younger daughter feels like she can't do anything that measures up. The well-behaved child thinks that the troublemaker gets all the attention. The first baby book is full of pictures; the fourth one is lucky to have the hospital photograph.

Families grow and change. Each addition changes the dynamics of the relationships. Temperaments mix or don't mix. Special needs or special situations arise. It's all normal.

And it's also normal for kids to try to figure out where they fit into it all. The self-conscious one wonders if you love her as much as the pretty one. The preschooler has a potty-training relapse when it seems like the new baby gets all the attention. One boy knows he'll never be the athlete his brother is, so he looks for another way to excel.

The one thing all kids have in common is the need to feel secure, to feel that they belong. Sometimes it's helpful to look at difficult behavior through this lens. Home should be the place where kids never have to worry if they fit in. Don't compare your kids to each other or try to relate to them in the same way on every point. Give the individual attention that assures them they belong—and that you're glad they're part of your family.

"He who fears the Lord has a secure fortress, and for his children it will be a refuge" (Proverbs 14:26).

Copyright © 2007 by Susan Martins Miller. Permission is granted to reproduce this page for ministry purposes only—not for resale.

I Don't Know What I Feel

You're giggling with your child and thinking what a wonderful moment this is, and in a split-second your son or daughter has crossed into the land of distress. What happened?

Kids' moods change constantly. With little ones, the slightest provocation can trigger a response you would not have thought possible—whether ecstasy or agony. Some of this has to do with basic temperament—the inborn traits your children use to react to the world. It may also be frustration. When kids don't understand what's happening or feel out of control of their environment, they get frustrated easily. And when they're frustrated, it seems like the reasonable side of their brains shut down.

Right from birth, kids experience a range of emotions. What they don't have are the words to identify what they're feeling. A tantrum may be rooted in anxiety—even for a teenager. Sullenness may have to do with disappointment. Exuberance may come from being picked to play on a team at school.

Help kids learn to label their feelings by acknowledging what they feel, rather than immediately trying to correct it. "I can see you're feeling scared." "That really disappointed you, didn't it?" "Wow, you're really proud of yourself!" Kids learn the words they need, but they also learn that you care. An emotional moment is the perfect time to remind kids that God cares too. Whatever happens to us, God is a safe place to take our feelings.

"Let the beloved of the Lord rest secure in him" (Deuteronomy 33:12).

Copyright © 2007 by Susan Martins Miller. Permission is granted to reproduce this page for ministry purposes only—not for resale.

Do As I Do

"Do as I say, not as I do." We laugh when we say that aloud because obviously that's not the way it works. We don't enjoy a double standard where we get to do whatever we want, but everybody else has to do the right thing.

Kids know it doesn't work that way too. Can you really tell your child to control his temper when he sees you lose yours on a regular basis? Can you insist that your child tell the truth all the time when she daily hears you bend the truth to suit your situation? Kids don't grow up to be honest, trustworthy, generous, and kind because someone told them those were good ideas. They develop those characteristics if they see them at work in their homes and communities.

You may not think your kids are paying attention. They are. They may not do everything you ask them to do, but they see everything that you do, and they're filing away mental notes. Later they pull out those notes and apply them in other situations. The white lie they heard you tell makes it all right for them to lie. The tone they heard you use with your spouse makes it all right for them to be disrespectful. The dusty, unused Bible they see on the shelf makes it all right for theirs to be under the bed.

"Do as I say, not as I do." Not really so funny.

"Set an example for the believers in speech, in life, in love, in faith and in purity" (1 Timothy 4:2).

Copyright © 2007 by Susan Martins Miller. Permission is granted to reproduce this page for ministry purposes only—not for resale.

Do You Remember?

Brent grumbled through the whole hike while his sister was having a great time. Mom and Dad planned a great vacation, but all the kids wanted to do was play video games. Choosing a Christmas tree together is a yearly squabble. Sometimes it just doesn't seem worth the effort.

But then you suggest making Christmas dinner without the rice pudding and meet protest on all fronts. Just when you're ready to give up, one of the kids asks where you're going on vacation this year.

Giving your kids a heritage may not be the picture-perfect experience it was supposed to be when you bought the book telling you how to do it. But that's all right. Most of the heritage comes from the unplanned moments you spend together. Make the most of everyday moments as well as special occasions.

Pretend you're rubber and bend in every direction. Go with the flow. When kids lose interest in decorating Christmas cookies after the first dozen, don't get cranky and insist they return to what has now become a chore. Enjoy the cookies that you did create together rather than lament the ones you didn't. In the everyday moments, ask yourself, "Is this the way I want my kids to remember me?" and adjust your mood and responses accordingly. Passing on a family heritage is not so much about creating moments as it is making the most of the ones you have together.

"Your statutes are my heritage forever; they are the joy of my heart" (Psalm 119:111).

Copyright © 2007 by Susan Martins Miller. Permission is granted to reproduce this page for ministry purposes only—not for resale.

When Someone Dies

Even adults don't understand death. Sure, we realize it's an inevitable part of our existence. But emotionally, we're still thrown for a loop. Imagine how much more difficult it is for a child to grasp the concept of death.

We're tempted to sugarcoat things. We think we're making it easier for children to deal with the death of a grandparent—or even a pet. But it's much better to tell the truth. Kids need to be sure the people who care for them will be truthful and reliable. That doesn't mean you have to tell all of the truth in one conversation. Watch your child carefully to see what he is absorbing and what questions arise. Answer the questions a child asks without feeling you must provide information the child did not ask for.

Remember that kids are watching you. How are you handling the loss? How are you responding to this new reality? Kids are taking their cues from you. Their attitudes will likely mirror yours.

"Why would God let this happen?" As adults we understand that sin and death came into the world when Adam and Eve chose to disobey God in the Garden of Eden. On an emotional level, that's not always enough of an answer. You don't have all the answers, and you don't have to pretend that you do. If your kids see you trusting in the love of God despite the circumstances, they'll want to do the same.

"Where, O death, is your victory? Where, O death, is your sting?" (1 Corinthians 15:55).

Copyright © 2007 by Susan Martins Miller. Permission is granted to reproduce this page for ministry purposes only—not for resale.

Are They Learning Anything?

What happened to the public school around the corner? It's still there, but today's parents have more choices than ever about where kids go to school. It's no longer a choice between just the local public school or forking out big money for private school.

Many school districts offer open enrollment, meaning parents can enroll a child in a school anywhere in the district. Magnet schools attract students with certain interests or abilities. Charter schools have distinctive philosophies that drive the curriculum. Home schooling has grown beyond levels anyone could have imagined a generation ago.

Even without paying the fees of private schools, parents have a spectrum of choices. So how do you know what's best for your child?

Remember, you are the one who knows your child best. You're the expert on the kind of environment you child enjoys learning in. You're the one who knows what stresses your child—or challenges or thrills. You can judge the kind of personality in teachers and administrators that is best for your child. You know your own philosophy about education. And you know what factors affect your family in terms of transportation, schedules, and finances.

The public school around the corner may still be the best choice for your family. Choosing it does not mean you settled for less than the best. The Lord knows what your child needs and will provide.

"Pay attention and listen to the sayings of the wise; apply your heart to what I teach" (Proverbs 22:17).

Copyright © 2007 by Susan Martins Miller. Permission is granted to reproduce this page for ministry purposes only—not for resale.

Is This Normal?

Lindy was walking at 10 months. When Hannah was 16 months old, her mother wondered if she was ever going to take a step. The preschool teacher sent a note home saying Jonathan needed "remedial scissors skills." Bailee could cut and paste with the pros. Bryan entered first grade reading fluently. In the second grade, Devon still struggled to put letters together and come up with the right sound.

What's "normal"? Experts in child development identify milestones that all kids reach, but they reach them at various times. Usually there is an age range for a milestone. It's normal for kids to develop on different time schedules. Remember that God creates every child, and God creates with astounding variety. So don't stress out if your child is not the first one on the block to ride a two-wheeler. Pay more attention to whether your child is developing the coordination and balance that will someday make him ready for the bike.

Sometimes kids do need extra help. If the rate of growth and development is not typical, meaning it does not fit into the range of what most kids do, don't hesitate to accept help. It's no one's fault if a child is dyslexic, for example, and the sooner the child gets extra help the better.

Don't judge your child's value by when she reaches a milestone. No matter where your child falls on the developmental spectrum, she is a precious creation of God, and God has a plan for your child's life.

"All the days ordained for me were written in your book before one of them came to be" (Psalm 139:16).

Copyright © 2007 by Susan Martins Miller. Permission is granted to reproduce this page for ministry purposes only—not for resale.

Introducing...

Faith that Sticks

Enhance learning and prompt a smile. Create a quick craft or inspire an idea.
Faith that Sticks™ stickers are a quick and whimsical resource or simply a way
to brighten a day!

Look for all these **Faith that Sticks**™ categories:

★ GOD MADE ★ BIBLE TIME

★ SMILE MAKER ★ FAITH SHAPES

★ GOD'S WORD ★ DAY BY DAY

Contact your Standard Publishing sales representative
or call 1-800-543-1353 for more information.

Standard
P U B L I S H I N G
Bringing The Word to Life™

126

Introducing...
The Storytelling Library
from
Steven James

FEATURING...

ALSO AVAILABLE . . .

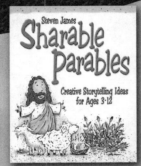

Recipient of the **Storytelling World Magazine Award** for 2003!

Crazy & Creative Bible Stories for Preteens
ISBN: 0-7847-1631-5
$15.99 (Can: $21.99)

Sharable Parables
Creative Storytelling Ideas for Ages 3–12
ISBN: 0-7847-1632-3
$15.99 (Can: $21.99)

The Creative Storytelling Guide for Children's Ministry
ISBN: 0-7847-1374-X
$19.99 (Can: $26.99)

2005 **Gold Medallion** Finalist!

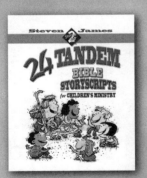

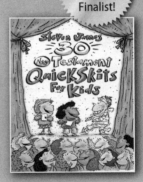

24 Tandem Bible StoryScripts for Children's Ministry
ISBN: 0-7847-1320-0
$15.99 (Can: $21.99)

24 Tandem Bible Hero StoryScripts for Children's Ministry
ISBN: 0-7847-1321-9
$15.99 (Can: $21.99)

30 Old Testament QuickSkits for Kids
ISBN: 0-7847-1629-3
$15.99 (Can: $21.99)

30 New Testament QuickSkits for Kids
ISBN: 0-7847-1630-7
$15.99 (Can: $21.99)

For more information, contact your Christian bookstore or visit us at www.standardpub.com

It's The **Heart** That Matters Most...

Standard Publishing HeartShaper Children's Curriculum

Standard PUBLISHING
Bringing The Word to Life
www.standardpub.com

Sunday School for Kids

www.heartshaper.com   For more information call **1-800-543-1353**